A-Z WINCHESTER

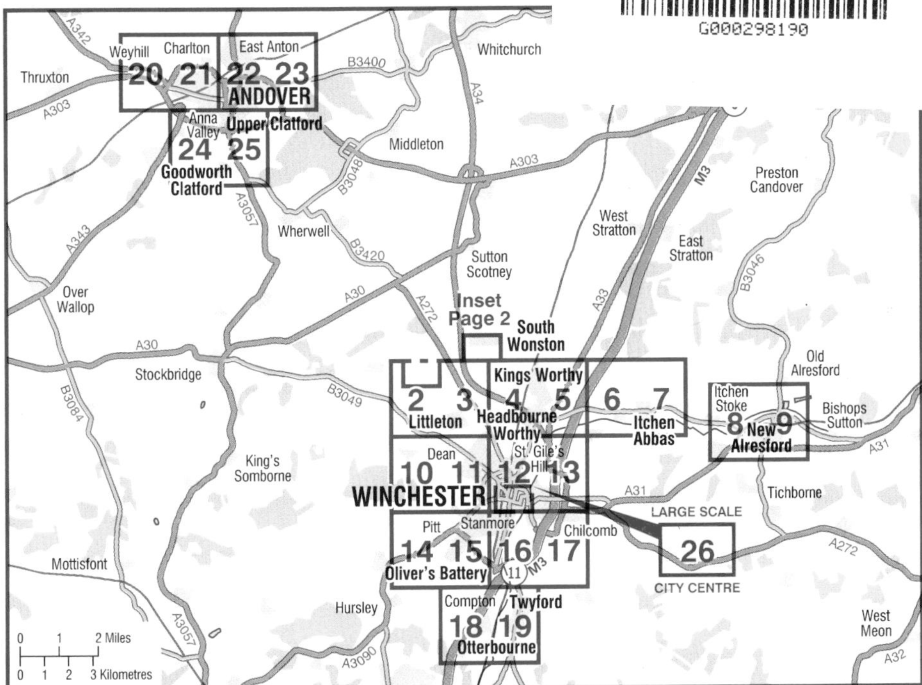

Reference

- **Motorway** M3
- **A Road** A33
- **B Road** B3040
- **Dual Carriageway**
- **One Way Street**
  Traffic flow on A roads is indicated by a heavy line on the driver's left.
  Large Scale Pages Only
- **Restricted Access**
- **Pedestrianized Road**
- **Track & Footpath**
- **Residential Walkway**
- **Railway** — Level Crossing, Station
- **Heritage Railway** — Station
- **Built Up Area** — WEST ST.
- **Local Authority Boundary**
- **Postcode Boundary**
- **Map Continuation** 12 — Large Scale City Centre 26
- **Car Park** Selected
- **Church or Chapel**
- **Fire Station**
- **Hospital**
- **House Numbers** A & B Roads only — 113, 98
- **Information Centre**
- **National Grid Reference** 450
- **Police Station**
- **Post Office**
- **Toilet**
  With facilities for the Disabled
- **Educational Establishment**
- **Hospital or Hospice**
- **Industrial Building**
- **Leisure or Recreational Facility**
- **Place of Interest**
- **Public Building**
- **Shopping Centre or Market**
- **Other Selected Buildings**

SCALES

Map Pages 2-25 1:15,840 4 inches to 1 mile

0 ¼ ½ Mile

0 250 500 750 Metres

6.31 cm to 1 km 10.16 cm to 1 mile

Map Page 26 1:7,920 8 inches to 1 mile

0 ⅛ ¼ Mile

0 100 200 300 Metres

12.63 cm to 1 km 20.32 cm to 1 mile

Geographers' A-Z Map Company Limited

Head Office :
Fairfield Road, Borough Green, Sevenoaks, Kent TN15 8PP
Tel: 01732 781000 (General Enquiries & Trade Sales)
Showrooms :
44 Gray's Inn Road, London WC1X 8HX
Tel: 020 7440 9500 (Retail Sales)
www.a-zmaps.co.uk

EDITION 2 2001

Crawley
Crawley Pond
Whitethorn House
Morns Field Cottages
Morns Field
SOUTH WONSTON
STAVEDOWN RD.
MARKSON RD.
STAINERS LA.
WRIGHTS CL.
KEATS CL.
BURNS
CHAUCER
LEONARDS CL.
ST.
GOLDFINCH WY.
Long Barrow
SPRUCE CL.
LONGBARROW CL.
WAVERLEY DR.
ROWAN CL.
W. HILL RD. NTH.
DOWNS ROAD
CHRISTMAS HILL
ORCHARD RD.
ORCHARD CL.
GROVES CL.
BLACKTHORN CL.
DOWNLANDS WY.
WALNUT TREE CL.
OAKLANDS
DOWNLANDS WAY
CHERRY CL.
South Wonston Prim. Sch.
LOVELL WY.
BORMAN CL.
ANDERS RD.
HUNT CL.
STRONG CL.
ARM
W. HILL RD. STH.
PADDOCK CL.
GREEN CL.
PINE
LOWER ROAD
Race Course Cottages
Pav.
Playing Field
Tennis Ct.
Playground
A34
SO21
BLACKWELL ROAD
INSET
3
4
Littleton House
Long Park
The Paddocks
Long Park Cottage
Long Park Farm
SO21
STOCKBRIDGE
B3049
Ball Down Service Station
Camping Site
Cradle Copse
Long Wood
Northwood Cottage
Winsley Cottage
NORTHWOOD PARK
Northwood Park Farm
Ball Down Farm
Sparsholt College
Garston Farm
Garstons Buildings
LANE
Telephone Exchange
Bushmoor Copse
Garston Cottages
Westley
WESTLEY
WATLEY LA.
Lodge
Lodge
ROAD
Water Tower
10
A
B
C
D
1
2
3
4
5
6
43
46
447
44
135
34
33
32

E
F
G
H
INSET
3
WORTHY DOWN
Worthy Grove
Roman Road
BLACKWELL RD.
BLACKWELL
REES RD.
MALPASS RD.
CONNAUGHT
COATE
BURNE CL.
DRIVE
COOPERS CL.
STANHAM CL.
COWLEY DR.
ROAD
Married Quarters
SOUTH WONSTON
WINCHESTER
A34
Gallop
Gas Valve Compound
A272
BY PASS
Down Farm
Underpass
DOWN FARM LANE
Lower Farm
Lower Farm Cottages
Lower Farm House
Drovers Way
Earthwork
Littleton Stud
Littleton Stud Cottages
Stud Lodge
Roman Road
CHURCH LANE
Littleton Manor
OLD STABLE MEWS
MAIN ROAD
SO22
B3420
ANDOVER ROAD
NORTH
NEW RD.
Tennis Court
Bowling Green
Pav.
Recreation Ground
Playground
Hall
ROZELLE CL.
HOLM OAK CL.
HOLLANDS CL.
THE HALL WY.
FAIR-CLOSE DR.
HILDEN WAY
FYFIELD WAY
PITTER CL.
WESTFIELD RD.
Nursery
UPHILL RD.
HILLTOP
LAWN RD.
HILLSIDE
FLOWERDOWN CARAVAN PARK
Tennis Cts.
SIR JOHN MOORE BARRACKS
Playing Field
LITTLETON
DALE CL.
VALLEY RD.
NORTH DRIVE
BERCOTE CL.
SOUTH DRIVE
KENNEL
DROVE
Flowerdown House
Telephone Exchange
Sewage Works
WELL HOUSE LA.
HARESTOCK CL.
HARESTOCK
PRIORS DEAN
BURITON
MINSTEAD CL.
GRAYSHOTT CL.
HICKORY DR.
ROAD
1
2
3
4
5
6
4
11
45
46
47
32
33
34
135

INSET PAGE 2
WORTHY DOWN CAMP
RILEY
ROAD
CONNAUGHT ROAD
STANHAM CL.
COWLEY DR.
STOKE
North Winchester Farm
Railway Cottages
CHARITY
Sewage Works
SO21
Down Farm
Underpass
WINCHESTER
DOWN FARM
A34
Woodhams Farm
CLOVER BANK ROAD
THE PASTURES
VALE WY.
KINGS CL.
ROBERTS CL.
CUNDELL
LARCH CL.
CEDAR CL.
WAY
MAPLE DR.
HOOKPIT FM. LA.
SYCAMORE DR.
FIRS CR.
ILEX CL.
LABURNUM DR.
ELIZABETH CL.
BROOKE CL.
FORBES
Springvale
TUDOR WY.
SO23
SPRINGVALE AV.
BENTLEY CL.
ST. NICHOLAS
SO22
Headbourne Worthy
Upper Farm
Vokes Cotts.
Watercress Beds
The White Cottage
Headbourne Worthy House
BEDFIELD LANE
TAYLORS CORNER
Manor House
GREEN CL.
LANE
SCHOOL LANE
Lower Farm
LONDON ROAD
PUDDING LA.
Sewage Works
ANDOVER ROAD NORTH
HARESTOCK CL.
WELL HOUSE LANE
Well House Farm
Headbourne Worthy Grange
GRAYSHOTT CL.
BEAULIEU CL.
STOCKBOURNE
A B C D
1 2 3 4 5 6
47 48 35 34 33 32
12
3

5
E
F
G
H
450
51
135
1
2
3
4
5
6
34
33
32
Depot
Southstoke Farm
Down Farm
Yearly Cotts.
Burntwood Cotts.
Burntwood Farm
Burntwood Cotts.
BRIDGETTS LANE
BASINGSTOKE ROAD
A33
Burntwood Cottages
Bull Farm
Bank Fm.
Copse Farm
Depot
Meadow Farm
SO21
ROMAN ROAD
9
M3
M3 MOTORWAY
Grace's Farm
Grace's Farm Cottages
B3047
EASTON LANE
MOUNTBATTEN PL.
SHERBROOKE CL.
POUND RD.
RAMSAY RD.
WESLEY RD.
TOVEY PL.
VIAN PL.
Rec. Grd.
SNIPES CL.
GILLINGHAM CL.
CEDARWOOD
HAMPTON WY.
LOADER CL.
Club
Recreation Ground
Playground
Hinton Cott.
FIELD END WAY
HOLDAWAY CL.
FELMER DR.
CAMPION
Kings Worthy Prim.Sch.
Hinton House
KINGS WORTHY
LANE
HINTON FIELDS
CHURCH LANE
THE WOODLANDS
Nursery
THE PADDOCK
Kingsworthy Ct.
COURT RD.
ST. MARY'S CL.
Hall
Works
NUNS WLK.
WEST FIELD RD.
The New House
Worthy Park
Homewood
WORTHY PARK
OLD RECTORY GDS.
PARK LANE
MILL LA.
Abbotsworthy House
ABBOTS WORTHY
Worthy Park Home Farm
The Worthys
Mill
Ford
Subway
RIVER ITCHEN
WATER LA.
Weir
Pumping Station
New Bridge Cott.
Easton Bridge
The Old Rectory
CHURCH LANE
THE TERRACE
MALTHOUSE CL.
EASTON
Hall
St. Mary Rector
Sports Grd.
Chapel
13

51
A
B
52
C
D
135
Rutherley Copse
Subway
Chillandham Farm
BRIDGETTS
CHILLANDHAM
1
Burntwood Cotts.
Rutherley Copse
M3
M3 MOTORWAY
Pavis Copse
Roman Villa (site of)
2
Reservoir (covered)
Bridget House
Bridget's Experimental Husbandry Farm
34
3
5
4
Chillandham Cottages
LANE
Couch Green
Garage Cottages
Grace's Farm
Grace's Farm Cottages
Martyr Worthy Place
COUCH GRN.
Rec. Grd.
Sports Grd.
P
Freefolk House
33
B3047
EASTON
Tel. Exchange
Cygnet House
Manor House
Martyr Worthy
CHURCH LANE
Hall
Chilland Barn
Upper Chilland House
5
Chilland
Chilland
Lower Chilland House
New Bridge Cott.
RIVER
ITCHEN
Easton Bridge
Weir
Pumping Station
6
Weir
Power House
Easton Lodge
AVINGTON LAKE
e Old ctory
CHURCH
LANE
THE TERRACE
EASTON
32
MALTHOUSE CL.
CHAPEL LA.
Hall
Earthwork
Sports Grd.
A
St. Mary's Rectory
B
C
D
51
52
EASTON
Low Grounds

Courtney's Copse
E
F
G
H
54
55
135
1
2
3
4
5
6
34
33
32
Oxdrove Way
ROAD
ITCHEN STOKE DOWN
New Cottages
Itchen Down Farm
Lone Farm
SO24
Spreadoak Cottages
Veterinary Centre
NORTHINGTON
RECTORY LANE
Rectory Lane Dairy
New Farm Cottages
SO21
Winton Cottages
BARING CL.
Abbey House
Railway Cottages
HAZELDENE GDS.
SCHOOL LA.
Little Hayes
LITTLE HAYES LANE
Clock Cottage
The Elms
ITCHEN ABBAS
STATION CL.
STATION APPROACH
OLD STATION RD.
Itchen Abbas Prim. Sch.
Itchen Abbas Ho.
STATION HILL
B3047
SHELLEY CL.
Works
Fish Farm
Park Farm
Itchen Abbas Manor
Chalk Pit
Waterfall
Avington Lodge
THE PARK GOLF COURSE
Avington House
The Pavilion
The Rectory
AVINGTON PARK
Yavington Farm Cottage
Club House
Earthwork
Pinder Centre
Lonsica
The New Houses
TEMPLE DR.
Yavington Farm
LOVINGTON LANE
Yavington Mead
The Row
Avington
West Hill Dairy

Dog Kennel Row
Watercress Beds
New House
Fobdown Farm
ABBOTSTONE RD
Watercress Beds
Oxdrove Way
Andover Water Plantation
Watercress Beds
Lodge
Folly Hill
Wind Pump
New England Cott.
Keepers Cott.
Fob Down
RIVER
Fish Farm
DROVE
Fish Pond
Arlebury Park
ITCHEN STOKE
Longcrate Cottages
Rectory
ITCHEN VW.
Manor Farm
Itchen Stoke Manor
Woodlands
West Lodge
Round House
B3047
WATER LA.
Itchen Stoke House
Garden Cottages
Watercress Beds
Borough Farm
WINCHESTER ROAD
LANE
NEW
DE-LUCY
AV.
BRIDGE
Cricket Grd.
Pav.
Church (site of)
Willowfield
Steward's Bri.
NICHOLSON PL.
SOUTH CL.
SOUTH
RIVER ITCHEN
B3047 ROAD
Fish Farm
FARM
DORIAN GRO.
JESTY RD.
Lady Croft Cottages
LADY CROFT
Ford
Itchenstoke Mill
ALRESFORD
COVEY
PERINS
Yew Tree Cottages
Lady Croft Farm
Watercress Beds
WATERCRESS MDW.
Ford
LOVINGTON LANE
Thatch Cottage
Hall
EAST LANE
Watercress Beds
KINGSLEY BNGS.
Park Farm
Ovington
ROAD
Pumping Sta.
Vernal Cotts.
A31
East Lodge
East Lane Cott.
East Lane Down
North Lodge
Ovington House
RIVER ITCHEN
South Lodge
Vernal Farm Cottage
Park Lodge
Vernal Farm
A31
ALRESFORD
Trodd's Copse
Winchester Lodge
The Crawls
56
57
34
33
32
31
A
B
C
D
1
2
3
4
5
6

OLD ALRESFORD
Sewage Wks.
GREEN CL.
KILN LANE
KILN LA.
Upton Park Farm
Ckt. Gd.
LANE
OX DROVE WAY
COLDEN
THE BROOK
The Lodge
Old Alresford Lodge
Rectory
Hill Ho.
Upton House
Gardener's Cott.
Wearne Ho.
Manor Farm
Old Alresford Place
Old Alresford Cott.
Watercress Beds
UPTON HOUSE
Lych Gate
Old Alresford House
B3046
OLD ALRESFORD PARK
Upton Lodge
Pinglestone Cottages
The Nythe House
Swan Cott.
Arle Mill
Pinglestone House
Weir House
Little Weir
Great Weir
Old Alresford Pond
Ladywell Ho.
LADY WELL LA.
MILL HILL
GREAT WEIR
THE SOKE
ALRE
NEW ALRESFORD
The Soke
ARLE CL.
THE
ARLE GDS.
HILL TER.
MALLARD CL.
VALDEAN MOBILE HOME PK.
Lib.
THE GEORGE YD.
BROAD ST.
Cardew Ho.
Arlebury Park Cotts.
Playground
Industrial Estate
Rec. Grd.
EVELYN MEWS
DEAN
THE SPINNEY CARAVAN PARK
Tennis Court
PARK MOUNT
WEST ST.
EAST ST.
BISHOPS SUTTON ROAD
Bensons
Langtons
Langton Gardens
Secundus
STATION RD.
BRANDY MT.
Cemy.
CHURCHYARD COTTS.
HAIG RD.
Langtons Lodge
Trees
The Lodge
AVENUE
POUND HILL
Alders Court
STATION APP.
Alresford
EDWARD TER.
(WATERCRESS LINE)
MID-HANTS RAILWAY
Perins Community Sch.
Tennis Ct.
Playing Field
ELLINGHAM CL.
ASH WK.
NURSERY ROAD
Watercress Beds
Western Court Farm
B3047
LANGTONS CT.
Langtons Farmhouse
BEECH
CHESTNUT WK.
LIME RD.
SEARLES CL.
ROAD
CARPENTERS
Hall
GRANGE
ROSEBERY RD
SALISBURY RD
B3046
HAWTHORN CL.
HILL
S024
Recreation Ground
ASHBURTON CL.
LOVELLS WK.
BRAMBLE
ELM RD.
MEADOW CL.
Chiltern Ct.
Makins Ct.
ROAD
Sun Hill Jun. & Inf. Schools
WINDSOR RD
ROBERTSON RD.
CULLEY VW.
GREEN
OAK
OAK HILL
FAWCETT CL.
WITTON HILL
BENENDEN
LINDLEY GDS.
BUTTERMERE GDS.
SUN HILL CRES.
MERYON
JACKLYNS CL.
MAPLE CL.
RUSSET CL.
Rec. Grd.
DERWENT GDS.
ENNERDALE GDS.
CONISTON GRO.
WATER GRO.
Depots
LINNETS
HASTED DR.
DICKENSON WK.
Pit (disused)
White Hill
LANE
Works
DOWN GA.
FAIRVIEW
DOWN
CORFE CL.
CARISBROOKE CL.
ORCHARD
WINDERMERE GDS.
CRES.
SPRING WY.
JACKLYNS
SHEPHERDS
ARUNDEL CL.
ROAD
DOVER CL.
APPLEDOWN CL.
PADDOCK WY.
Bell House
GDS.
TICHBORNE DOWN
WHITEHILL
A31
Sunny View
Thistledown
APPLEDOWN LANE
TICHBORNE DOWN
ALRESFORD GOLF COURSE
Club House
B3046
Pit (disused)
Hassock's Copse
E
F
G
H
1
2
3
4
5
6
59
460
34
33
32
131
8

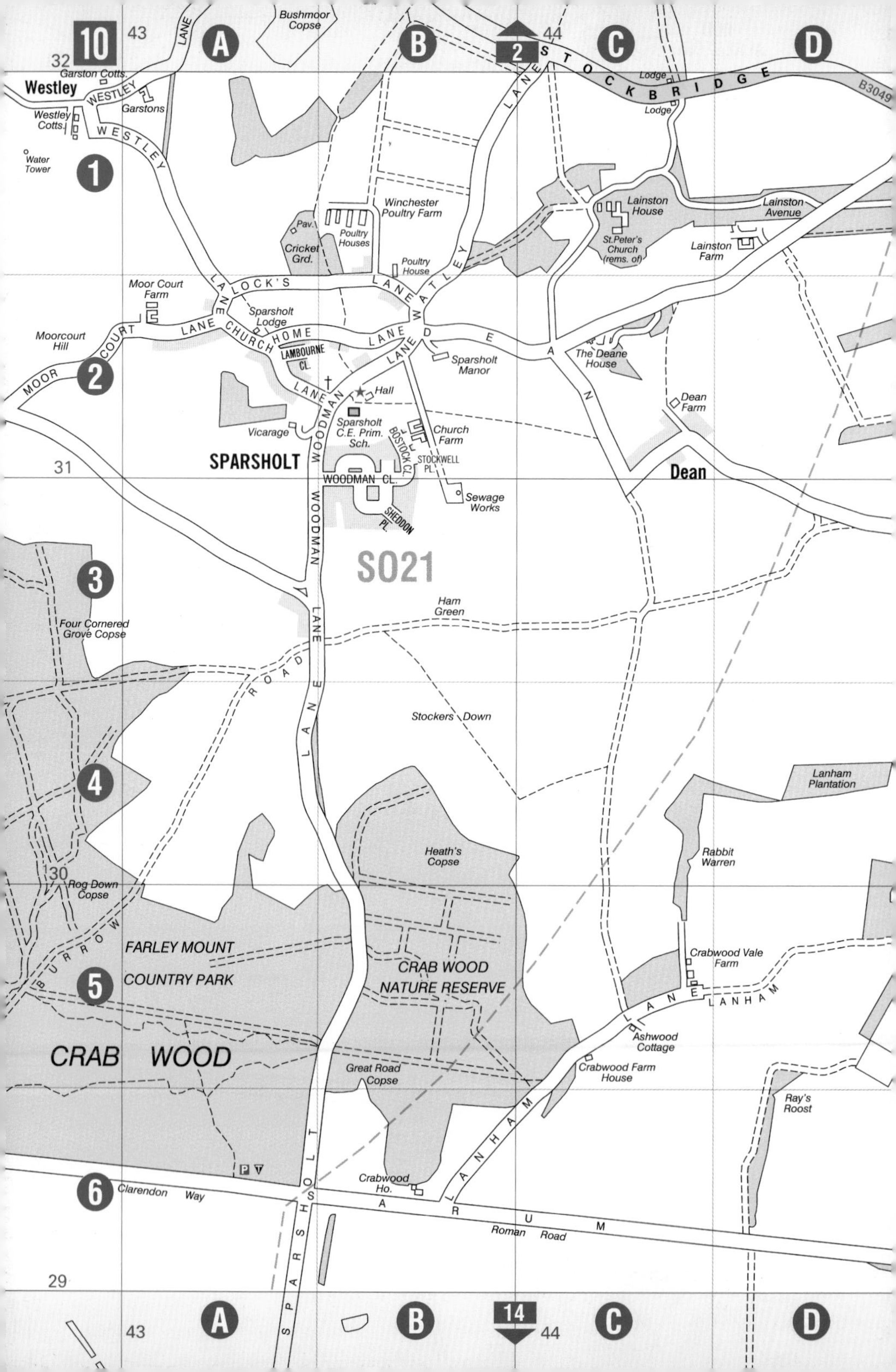
10
43
44
A
B
C
D
1
2
3
4
5
6
32
31
30
29
14
Westley
Garston Cotts.
Westley Cotts.
Garstons
Water Tower
WESTLEY
LANE
Bushmoor Copse
STOCKBRIDGE
B3049
Lodge
Lodge
Lainston House
Lainston Avenue
St.Peter's Church (rems. of)
Lainston Farm
Winchester Poultry Farm
Poultry Houses
Poultry House
Pav.
Cricket Grd.
WATLEY LANE
LOCK'S LANE
Moor Court Farm
Moorcourt Hill
MOOR COURT LANE
Sparsholt Lodge
CHURCH LANE
HOME LANE
LAMBOURNE CL.
DEAN LANE
The Deane House
Sparsholt Manor
Hall
Sparsholt C.E. Prim. Sch.
Vicarage
Church Farm
BOSTOCK CL.
STOCKWELL PL.
SPARSHOLT
WOODMAN CL.
WOODMAN LANE
SHEDDON PL.
Sewage Works
Dean Farm
Dean
SO21
Four Cornered Grove Copse
Ham Green
BURROW ROAD
Stockers Down
Lanham Plantation
Rabbit Warren
Heath's Copse
Rog Down Copse
FARLEY MOUNT COUNTRY PARK
CRAB WOOD NATURE RESERVE
CRAB WOOD
Crabwood Vale Farm
LANHAM LANE
Ashwood Cottage
Crabwood Farm House
Great Road Copse
Ray's Roost
Crabwood Ho.
Clarendon Way
ARUM
Roman Road
SPARSHOLT

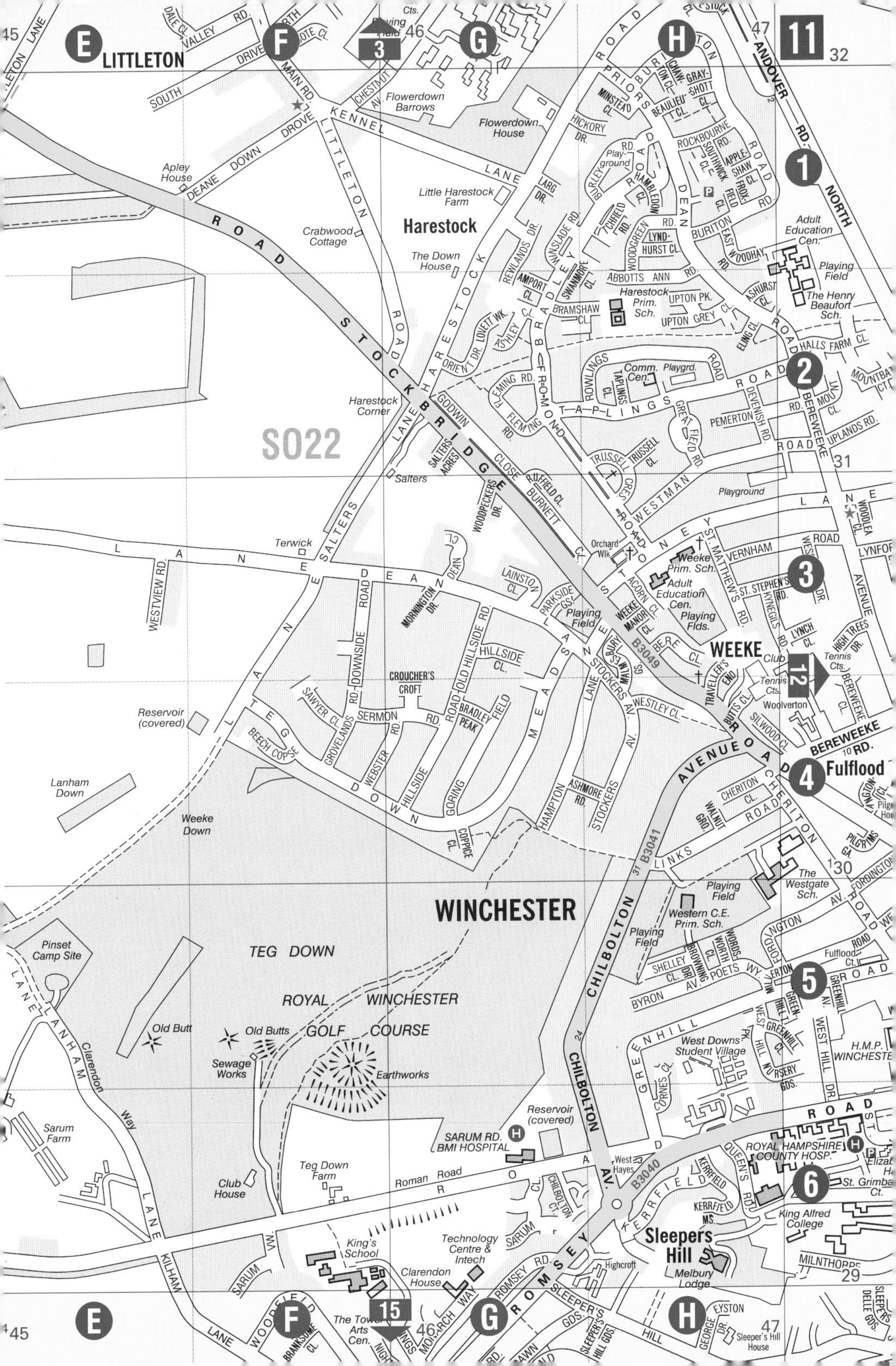
11
E
F
G
H
1
2
3
4
5
6
3
12
15
45
46
47
32
31
30
29
LITTLETON
Harestock
WEEKE
Fulflood
WINCHESTER
Sleepers Hill
SO22
TEG DOWN
ROYAL WINCHESTER GOLF COURSE
STOCKBRIDGE ROAD
ANDOVER RD. NORTH
CHILBOLTON AVENUE
ROMSEY RD.
B3049
B3041
B3040
DEANE DOWN DROVE
KENNEL LANE
LITTLETON ROAD
HARESTOCK ROAD
PRIORS DEAN ROAD
BRADLEY RD.
TAPLINGS ROAD
FROMOND RD.
WESTMAN ROAD
STONEY LANE
DEAN LANE
SALTERS LANE
TEG DOWN MEADS
DOWNSIDE ROAD
TEG DOWN
BEREWEEKE ROAD
BEREWEEKE AVENUE
CHERITON ROAD
LINKS ROAD
GREENHILL ROAD
ROMAN ROAD
SARUM RD.
LANHAM LANE
KILHAM LANE
Clarendon Way
KERRFIELD
SLEEPER'S HILL
WESTVIEW RD.
Flowerdown Barrows
Flowerdown House
Apley House
Little Harestock Farm
Crabwood Cottage
The Down House
Harestock Corner
Salters
Terwick
Harestock Prim. Sch.
Comm. Cen.
Playgrd.
Playground
Adult Education Cen.
Playing Field
The Henry Beaufort Sch.
Weeke Prim. Sch.
Playing Flds.
Tennis Cts.
Woolverton
Club
Reservoir (covered)
Lanham Down
Weeke Down
The Westgate Sch.
Western C.E. Prim. Sch.
West Downs Student Village
H.M.P. WINCHESTER
Pinset Camp Site
Old Butt
Old Butts
Sewage Works
Earthworks
Sarum Farm
Club House
Teg Down Farm
SARUM RD. BMI HOSPITAL
West Hayes
ROYAL HAMPSHIRE COUNTY HOSP.
King Alfred College
St. Grimbald Ct.
King's School
Technology Centre & Intech
Clarendon House
The Tower Arts Cen.
Highcroft
Melbury Lodge
Sleeper's Hill House
CROUCHER'S CROFT
Orchard Wlk.
Fulflood Ct.

A
B
C
D
1
2
3
4
5
6
4
26
11
16
S022
S023
WINCHESTER
Abbotts Barton
Hyde
Fulflood
WEEKE
West Hill
The Close
The Soke
Wharf Hill
ANDOVER ROAD
NORTH
B3420
LONDON ROAD
WORTHY ROAD
B3047
WELL HOUSE LANE
STONEY LANE
PARK ROAD
BEREWEEKE ROAD
B3044
STOCKBRIDGE ROAD
B3049
ROMSEY ROAD
B3040
HIGH ST.
NORTH WALLS
FRIARSGATE
ST. GEORGE'S ST.
JEWRY ST.
CITY RD.
UPPER HIGH ST.
Well House Farm
Headbourne Worthy Grange
Barton Mark
Waterside
Barton Hill Farm Cottages
Lower Farm
Barton Farm
Barton Cotts.
Adult Education Cen.
Playing Field
The Henry Beaufort Sch.
ST.WALERIC HOSPITAL
Winton House
Greenacres Sch.
Brooks Sch.
Lankhills School
Peter Symonds' College
Nethercliffe Sch.
Swim. Pool
Abbotts Barton Fm. Ho.
Rugby Football Ground
Athletic Ground
North Walls Recreation Ground
River Park Leisure Cen.
Riverside Indoor Rec. Bowl. Club
Winnall Moors Nature Reserve
Winchester Gallery
Winchester Sch. of Art
St. Bede C.E. Prim. Sch.
The Westgate Sch.
Western C.E. Prim. Sch.
West Downs Student Village
H.M.P. WINCHESTER
ROYAL HAMPSHIRE COUNTY HOSPITAL
St. Grimbald's Ct.
King Alfred College
Cemetery
Oram's Arbour Rec. Grd.
County Council Offs.
Peninsula Barracks
CATHEDRAL
Visitor Cen.
Deanery
The Pilgrims Sch.
Wolvesey Castle
Wolvesey Palace
Winchester Coll.
St. Mary Magdalen Almshouses
Tumbling Bay
ST. MARTINS TRADE PARK
Winchester

13
5
17
E
F
G
H
1
2
3
4
5
6
50
51
49
32
31
30
29
Pumping Station
Weir
Weir
CHURCH
LANE
THE TERRACE
MALT HOUSE CL.
CHAPEL LANE
Hall
Sports Grd.
Chapel Field
Cockets Mead
EASTON DOWN
M3 MOTORWAY
M3
Dairy Farm
Dairy Cottages
Easton Manor Farm
Lone Barn
EASTON LANE
LONG WALK
Winnall Cottage Farm
White Hill Cott.
Shoulder of Mutton Farm
Harfield Farm
WINCHESTER BY-PASS
A33
Works
Depot
ITCHEN
RIVER
THE WYKEHAM INDUSTRIAL ESTATE
THE WYKHAM INDUSTRIAL ESTATE
Gasholder Sta.
Warehouse
Junction 9
SPITFIRE LINK
SO21
MOORSIDE ROAD
LEICESTER WAY
MOORSIDE
Works
Depot
WINNALL TRADING EST.
Superstore
ERASMUS PARK
WINNALL CL.
Craddock Ho.
Braxton Ho.
Dennett Ho.
Earle Ho.
Winnall Down Copse
Winnall Down Farm
Roseacre
WINNALL TRADING ESTATE
WINNALL VALLEY RD.
Works
LONGFIELD RD.
WARREN RD.
MANOR ROAD
Winnall
IMBER
GARBETT RD
Comm. Cen.
Winnall Prim. Sch.
SHEPHERDS
LONGFIELD
GOY GN RD.
FIRMSTONE RD.
BAIGENT CL.
WINNALL
TURNPIKE
GATEKPR CL.
LONGHO. GRN
LIMETREE WK.
Fairdown
HUTS RSE.
ROUND
PEACOCK PL.
RINGLET WY.
DOWN END
SPITFIRE
A272
Tennis Cts.
St. Swithun's School
No Man's Land
FAIR LANE
Magdalen Hill Farm
Glencross
ALRESFORD ROAD
B3404
Cemy.
NORTHBROOK CL.
NORTHBROOK CT.
FAIRDOWN CL.
ROAD
BROOK AV.
St. Giles's Hill
CHALK RIDGE
ROAD
MAGDALEN HILL DOWN
Works
Lodge
Magdalen Hill Cemetery
PETERSFIELD ROAD
A31
KINGS LA.
FIVEFIELDS
ST. LEONARD'S RD.
NELSON RD.
FIVE FIELDS CL.
AVENUE ROAD
GORDON
Highcliffe
Rec. Grd.
ST. CATHERINES WAY

43
A
B
Roman Road
10
44
C
D
29
1
2
3
4
5
6
28
27
26
LANE
ENMILL LANE
Enmill House
Enmill Bungalow
Enmill Barn
Enmill Cottage
Enmill Farm
Pit View
Vale Farm
The Strawberry Fields
Sunbeam
White House
A3090
Yew Tree
ROMSEY
Reservoir (covered)
MILLERS
Pitt Copse
Grovelands Copse
Stopham's Copse
Larkfarm Plantation
SHOLT
FARLEY MT. RD.
SPARSHOLT
Standon Fm.
Standon
Juniper Bank
Nan Trodd's Hill
Butcher's Plantation
SO21
Down Farm
Chalk Pit
PORT
A
B
43
44
C
D

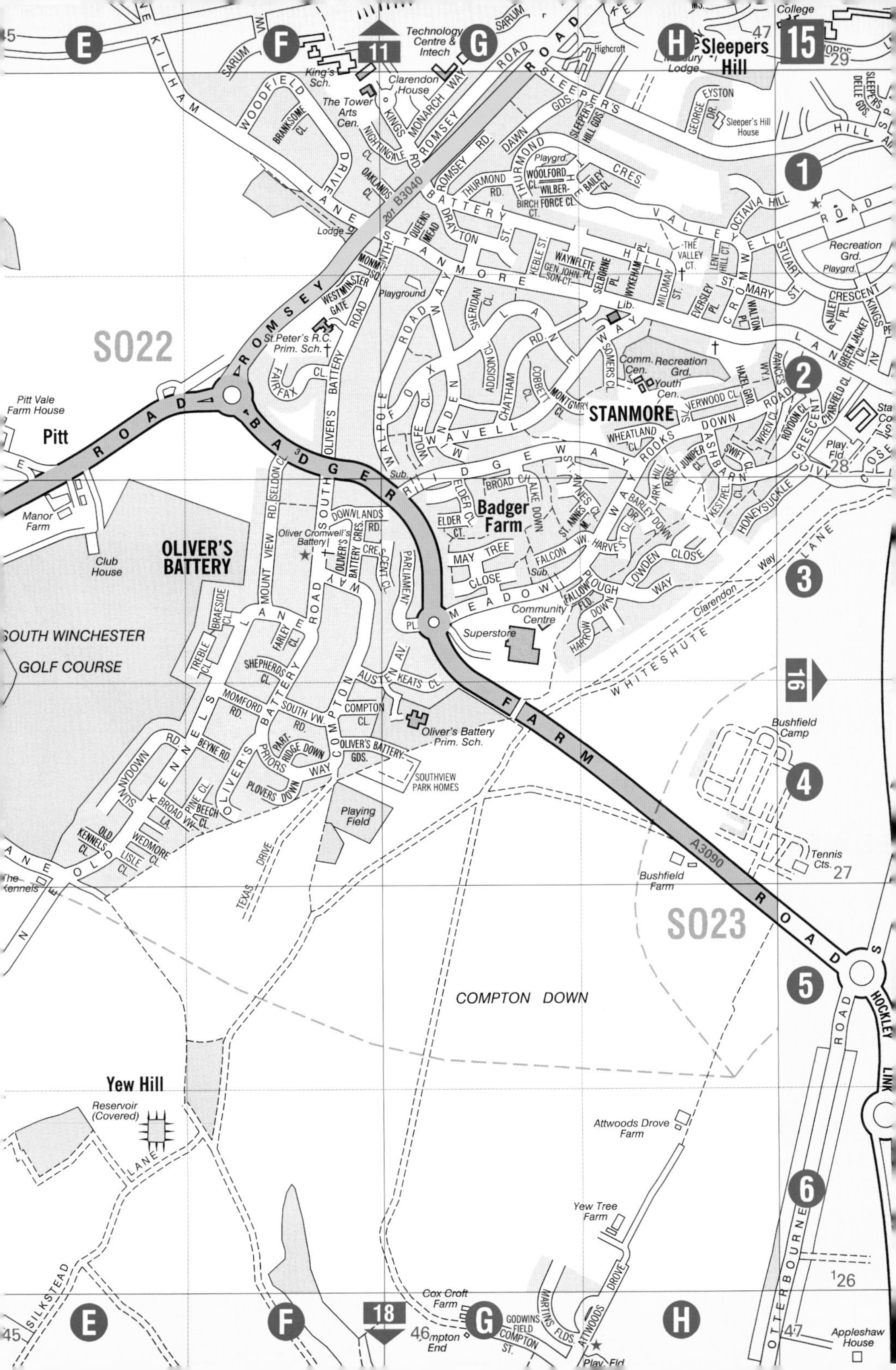

11
15
16
18
Sleepers Hill
STANMORE
Badger Farm
OLIVER'S BATTERY
Pitt
Yew Hill
SO22
SO23
SOUTH WINCHESTER
GOLF COURSE
COMPTON DOWN
ROMSEY ROAD
BADGER FARM ROAD
A3090
B3040
Technology Centre & Intech
King's Sch.
Clarendon House
The Tower Arts Cen.
Sleeper's Hill House
Recreation Grd.
St.Peter's R.C. Prim. Sch.
Pitt Vale Farm House
Manor Farm
Club House
Oliver Cromwell's Battery
Comm. Cen.
Youth Cen.
Community Centre
Superstore
Oliver's Battery Prim. Sch.
SOUTHVIEW PARK HOMES
Playing Field
Bushfield Camp
Bushfield Farm
Tennis Cts.
Reservoir (Covered)
Attwoods Drove Farm
Yew Tree Farm
Cox Croft Farm
Appleshaw House
The Kennels
WHITESHUTE LANE
Clarendon Way
OTTERBOURNE ROAD
HOCKLEY LINK

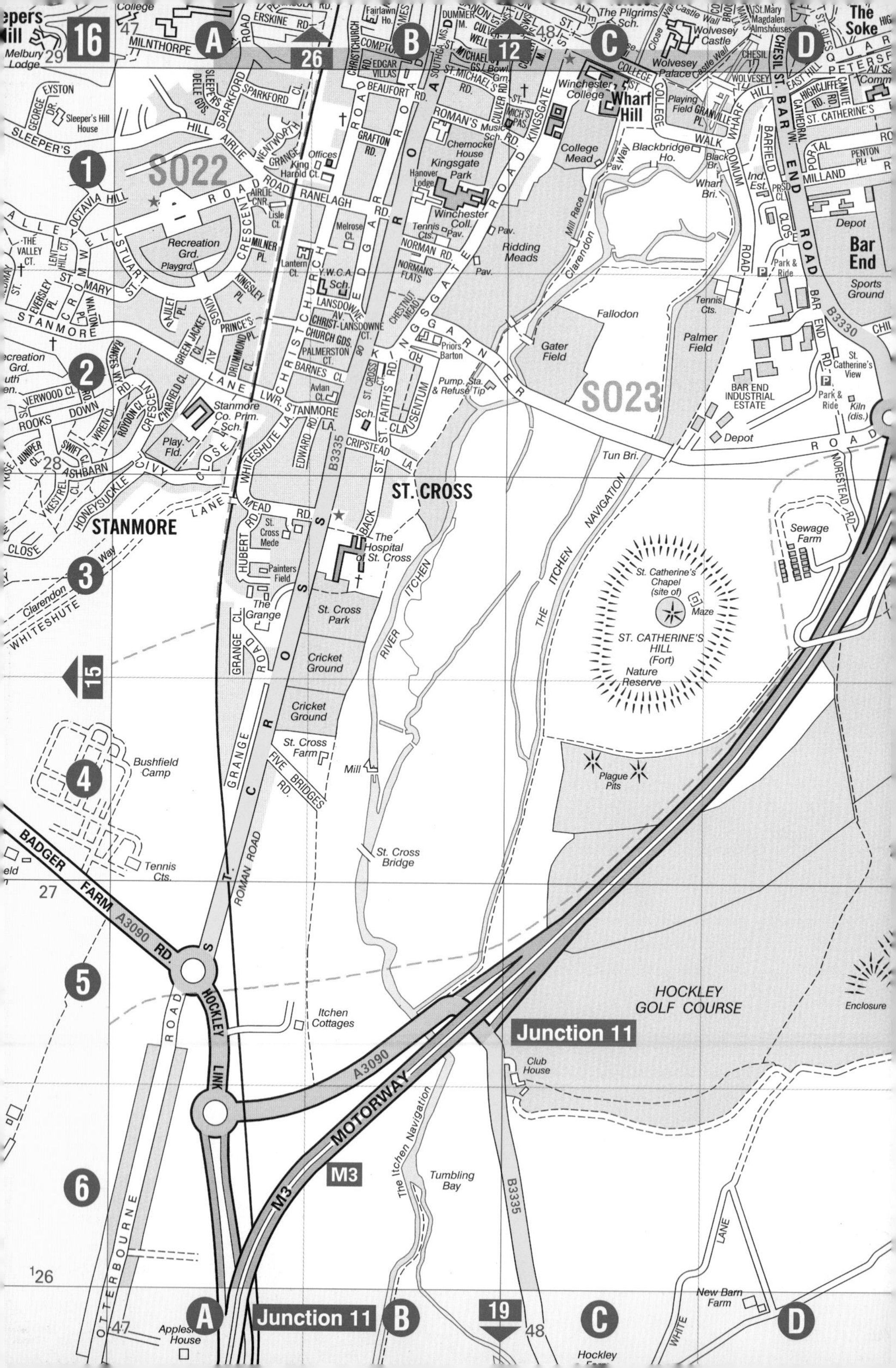

Sleepers Hill
Melbury Lodge
A
B
C
D
26
12
Junction 11
19
15
1
2
3
4
5
6
SO22
SO23
ST. CROSS
STANMORE
The Soke
Wharf Hill
Bar End
Winchester College
Wolvesey Castle
Wolvesey Palace
The Pilgrims Sch.
St.Mary Magdalen Almshouses
Kingsgate Park
Winchester Coll.
Ridding Meads
College Mead
Recreation Grd.
Playgrd.
Stanmore Co. Prim. Sch.
Play. Fld.
Sleeper's Hill House
The Hospital of St. Cross
St. Cross Park
Cricket Ground
St. Cross Farm
Mill
St. Cross Bridge
Bushfield Camp
Tennis Cts.
Itchen Cottages
Fallodon
Gater Field
Palmer Field
Tun Bri.
Pump. Sta. & Refuse Tip
Priors Barton
BAR END INDUSTRIAL ESTATE
Depot
Sports Ground
Park & Ride
Kiln (dis.)
St. Catherine's View
Sewage Farm
St. Catherine's Chapel (site of)
Maze
ST. CATHERINE'S HILL (Fort)
Nature Reserve
Plague Pits
HOCKLEY GOLF COURSE
Enclosure
Club House
Tumbling Bay
New Barn Farm
Hockley
Applesh House
RIVER ITCHEN
THE ITCHEN NAVIGATION
The Itchen Navigation
Clarendon Way
M3 MOTORWAY
A3090
B3335
B3330
BADGER FARM RD.
HOCKLEY LINK
OTTERBOURNE ROAD
ROMAN ROAD
GRANGE RD.
ST. CROSS RD.
FIVE BRIDGES RD.
CHRISTCHURCH RD.
SOUTHGATE ST.
KINGSGATE RD.
KINGSGATE ST.
EDGAR RD.
ST. FAITH'S RD.
CLAUSENTUM RD.
BACK ST.
CRIPSTEAD LA.
MEAD RD.
HUBERT RD.
WHITESHUTE LA.
STANMORE LANE
LWR. STANMORE LA.
ST. JAMES LANE
AIRLIE RD.
RANELAGH RD.
CROMWELL RD.
STUART CRES.
KINGS AV.
CIVIC WAY
HONEYSUCKLE CLOSE
GARNIER RD.
BAR END RD.
CHESIL ST.
DOMUM RD.
WHARF HILL
COLLEGE WALK
COLLEGE ST.
MORESTEAD RD.
WHITE LANE
ST. CATHERINE'S
MILLAND
PETERSFIELD
CATHEDRAL VW.
CANUTE RD.
HIGHCLIFFE RD.
EAST HILL
BARFIELD CLOSE
BEAUFORT RD.
GRAFTON RD.
NORMAN RD.
ROMAN'S RD.
CULVER RD.
ST. MICHAEL'S RD.
EDGAR VILLAS
COMPTON RD.
ERSKINE RD.
MILNTHORPE RD.
SPARKFORD RD.
SLEEPER'S HILL
EYSTON
GEORGE DR.
OCTAVIA HILL
STANMORE
ROOKS DOWN
JUNIPER CL.
ASHBARN
KESTREL
WREN CL.
SWIFT CL.
ROYDON CL.
CHARFIELD CL.
GREEN JACKET CL.
DRUMMOND CL.
PRINCE'S
KINGSLEY PL.
MILNER PL.
PAULET PL.
LANSDOWNE AV.
CHRIST-CHURCH GDS.
PALMERSTON CT.
BARNES CL.
Avlan Ct.
Sch.
Y.W.C.A. Sch.
Lantern Ct.
Melrose Ct.
Lisle Ct.
King Harold Ct.
Offices
Hanover Lodge
Chernocke House
Music Sch.
Tennis Cts.
Pav.
NORMANS FLATS
CHESTNUT MEAD
St. Cross Mede
Painters Field
The Grange
Blackbridge Ho.
Black Br.
Wharf Bri.
Mill Race
Playing Field
GRANVILLE PL.
Ind. Est.
Fairlawn Ho.
29
28
27
1 26
47
48

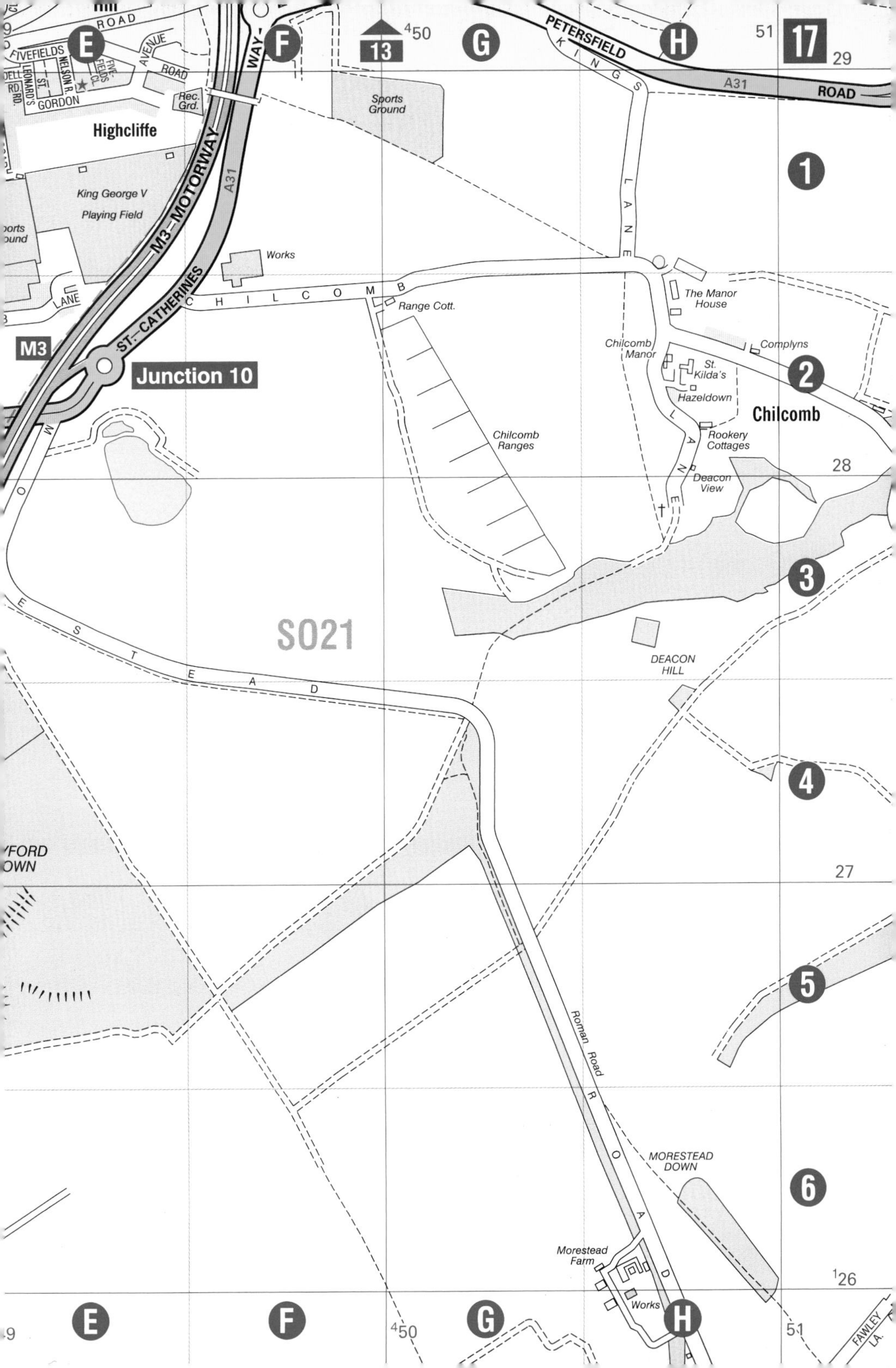

ROAD
FIVEFIELDS
NELSON R.
FIVE-FIELDS CL.
AVENUE
ROAD
ST. LEONARD'S RD.
GORDON
Rec. Grd.
Highcliffe
WAY
E
F
13
450
G
PETERSFIELD
KINGS LANE
H
51
17
29
A31
ROAD
Sports Ground
King George V
Playing Field
M3–MOTORWAY
A31
Works
CHILCOMB
Range Cott.
ST. CATHERINES
LANE
M3
Junction 10
The Manor House
Complyns
Chilcomb Manor
St. Kilda's
Hazeldown
Chilcomb
Rookery Cottages
Chilcomb Ranges
Deacon View
LANE
28
MORESTEAD
SO21
DEACON HILL
YFORD OWN
27
Roman Road
ROAD
MORESTEAD DOWN
Morestead Farm
Works
126
FAWLEY LA.
1
2
3
4
5
6
E
F
G
H
49
450
51

A
B
C
D
15
445
46
26
125
24
23
1
2
3
4
5
6
Yew Tree Farm
Cox Croft Farm
Compton End
COMPTON
GODWINS FIELD
MARTINS FLDS.
ATTWOODS DROVE
Play. Fld.
LANE
Church Farm
STREET
CARMANS LA.
Compton C.E. Prim. School
WINCHESTER
WELSHERS
HURDLE
Compton
WAY
SILKSTEAD
LANE
Compton Down
CLEASE WAY
THE SPINNEY
FIELD CLOSE
FIELD
Playing Field
Tennis Cts.
Pav.
CLIFF LANE
OTTERBOURNE ROAD
New Barn Farm
SHEPHERDS LANE
SHEPHERDS
Silkstede Priors
Upper Silkstead Farm
Four Dell Farm
Shepherds Down School
Sub.
SOUTHDOWN ROAD
TILDEN RD.
South Down
Windrush Cottage
Highways Poultry Farm
HIGHWAYS RD.
Southdown Grange
POLES
Otterbourne Golf Centre
Dean Copse
Dean Croft
Woodlands
Nursery
FAIRFIELD
CROSSWAYS ROAD
GROVE RD.
GROVE RD.
SOUTHDOWN ROAD
Sandhill
Freemantles Copse
The Bungalow
Refuse Incineration Plant
Poles Copse
LANE
COPSE CL.
SPARROWGROVE
Sparrowgrove Copse
RICHMOND PK.
WATERWORKS ROAD
REGENT CL.
NORLANDS DR.
BOURNE CL.
MAIN ROAD
Oakwood Ho.
Oakwood Copse
OAKWOOD CL.
OAKWOOD AV.
Matthew's Copse
MEADOWCROFT CL.
Recreation Ground
Water Works
M3 MOTORWAY
M3
CRANBOURNE DR.
OLD PARSONAGE CT.
GREENACRES DR.
BROOKLYN CL.
Pavilion
Hessians Copse
CRANBURY PARK
Great Moorlands Copse
COLES MEDE
DRIVE
Forge Bungalow
Roman Road
COLES MEDE
MEWS CT.
CRANBURY CL.
CRANBOURNE
MAIN
Village Hall
Otterbourne
Otterbourne Ho.
OTTERBOURNE HOUSE GDS.
Dell Copse
Otterbourne C.E.Prim. Sch.

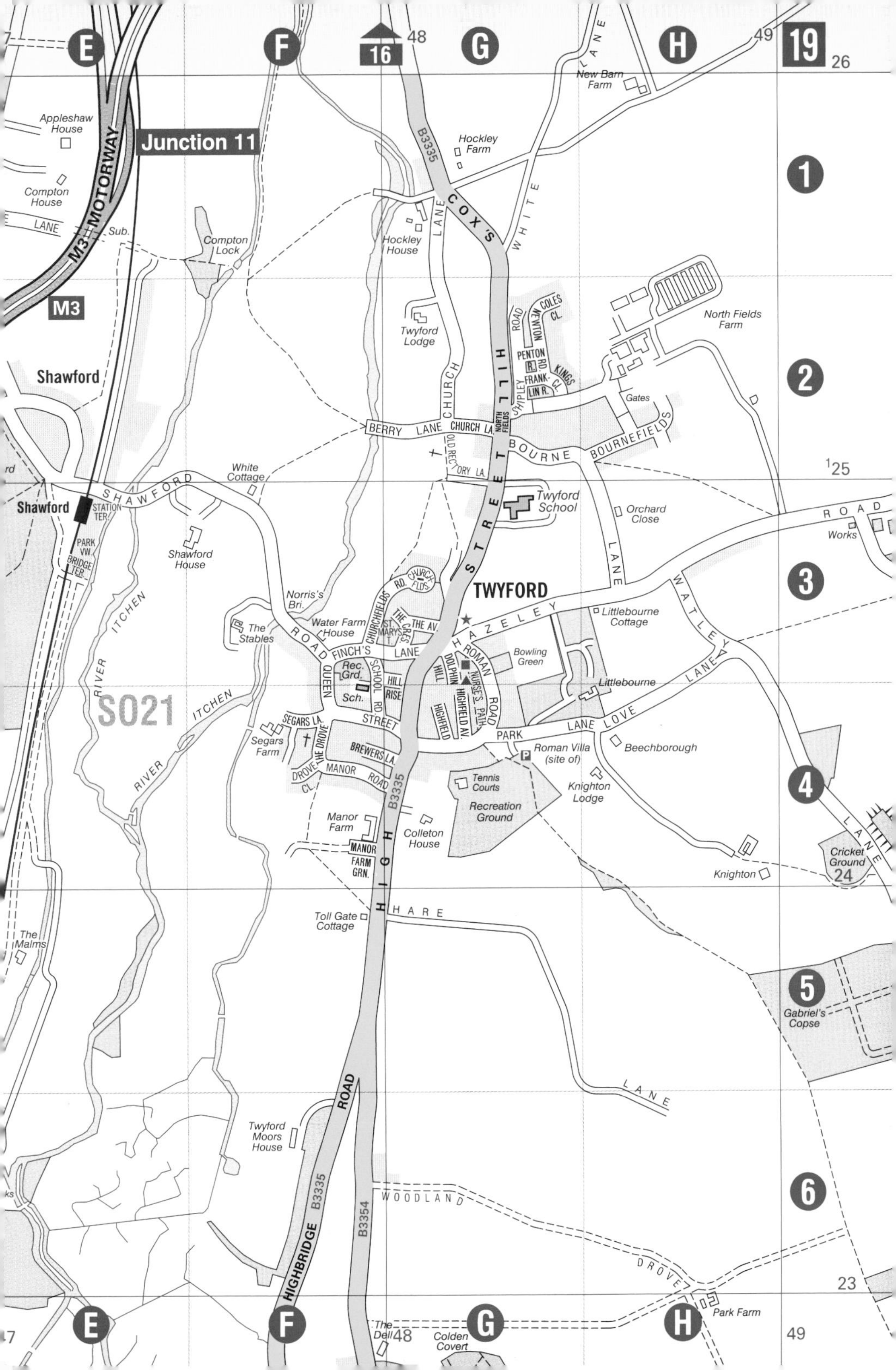
Junction 11
M3 MOTORWAY
M3
Appleshaw House
Compton House
LANE
Sub.
Compton Lock
Shawford
Shawford
STATION TER.
PARK VW.
BRIDGE TER.
SHAWFORD
White Cottage
Shawford House
Norris's Bri.
The Stables
ROAD
RIVER ITCHEN
S021
Segars Farm
SEGARS LA.
THE DROVE
DROVE CL.
MANOR ROAD
BREWERS LA.
Manor Farm
MANOR FARM GRN.
Colleton House
Toll Gate Cottage
HARE LANE
Twyford Moors House
HIGHBRIDGE ROAD
B3335
B3354
WOODLAND DROVE
The Dell
Colden Covert
Park Farm
The Malms
Hockley Farm
Hockley House
Twyford Lodge
COX'S HILL
HIGH STREET
CHURCH LANE
BERRY LANE
CHURCH LA.
NORTH FIELDS
OLD RECTORY LA.
Twyford School
TWYFORD
CHURCHFIELDS RD.
CHURCH FLDS.
THE CRES.
THE AV.
ST. MARYS T.
Water Farm House
FINCH'S LANE
Rec. Grd.
Sch.
SCHOOL RD.
QUEEN STREET
HILL RISE
DOLPHIN HILL
ROMAN ROAD
NURSE'S PATH
HIGHFIELD AV.
HIGHFIELD
Bowling Green
HAZELEY ROAD
PARK LANE
LOVE LANE
Roman Villa (site of)
Tennis Courts
Recreation Ground
Knighton Lodge
Beechborough
Littlebourne
Littlebourne Cottage
WATLEY LANE
Knighton
Cricket Ground
Gabriel's Copse
WHITE LANE
New Barn Farm
North Fields Farm
ROAD
NEWTON COLES CL.
PENTON RD.
SHIPLEY
FRANK. CL.
LIN R.
KINGS
Gates
BOURNE
BOURNEFIELDS
Orchard Close
Works
LANE
16
E
F
G
H
1
2
3
4
5
6
48
49
26
25
24
23
47

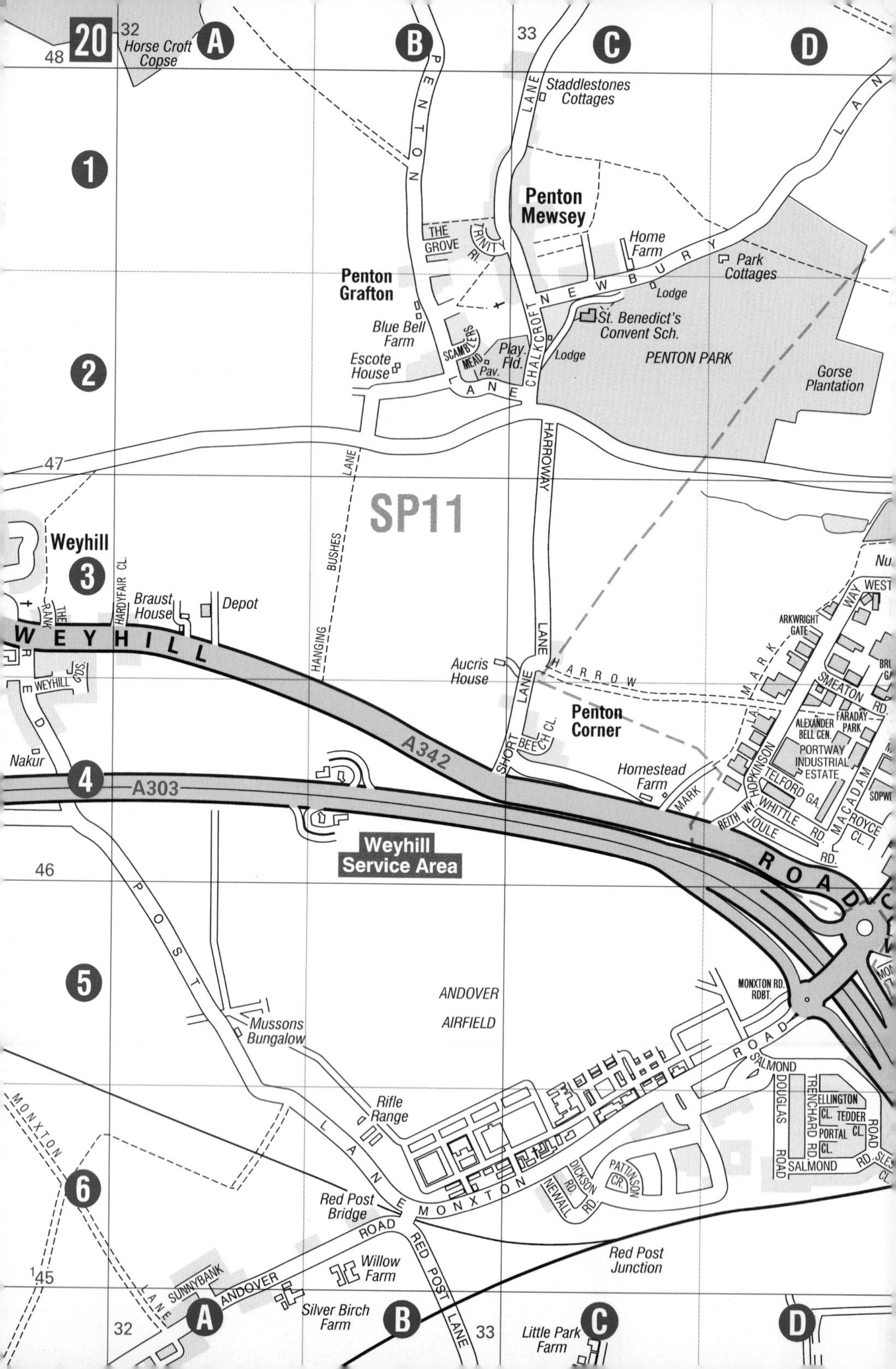
20
A
B
C
D
1
2
3
4
5
6
32
33
48
47
46
45
Horse Croft Copse
Staddlestones Cottages
Penton Mewsey
Home Farm
Park Cottages
Lodge
St. Benedict's Convent Sch.
PENTON PARK
Gorse Plantation
Penton Grafton
Blue Bell Farm
Escote House
Play. Fld.
Pav.
THE GROVE
TRINITY RI.
SCAMBLERS MEAD
PENTON LANE
CHALKCROFT LANE
NEWBURY LANE
HARROWAY
SP11
Weyhill
HARDYFAIR CL.
THE RANK
Braust House
Depot
WEYHILL
WEYHILL GDS.
HANGING BUSHES LANE
Aucris House
HARROW WAY
Penton Corner
BEECH CL.
SHORT LANE
Homestead Farm
A342
A303
Nakur
Weyhill Service Area
ARKWRIGHT GATE
SMEATON RD.
ALEXANDER BELL CEN.
FARADAY PARK
PORTWAY INDUSTRIAL ESTATE
HOPKINSON
TELFORD GA.
WHITTLE RD.
JOULE RD.
REITH WY.
MACADAM
ROYCE CL.
MARK LANE
ROAD
ANDOVER AIRFIELD
MONXTON RD. RDBT.
POST LANE
Mussons Bungalow
Rifle Range
MONXTON ROAD
SALMOND
DOUGLAS ROAD
TRENCHARD RD.
ELLINGTON CL.
TEDDER CL.
PORTAL CL.
DICKSON RD.
NEWALL RD.
PATTINSON CR.
Red Post Bridge
ANDOVER ROAD
RED POST LANE
Willow Farm
Red Post Junction
SUNNYBANK
LANE
Silver Birch Farm
Little Park Farm
MONXTON

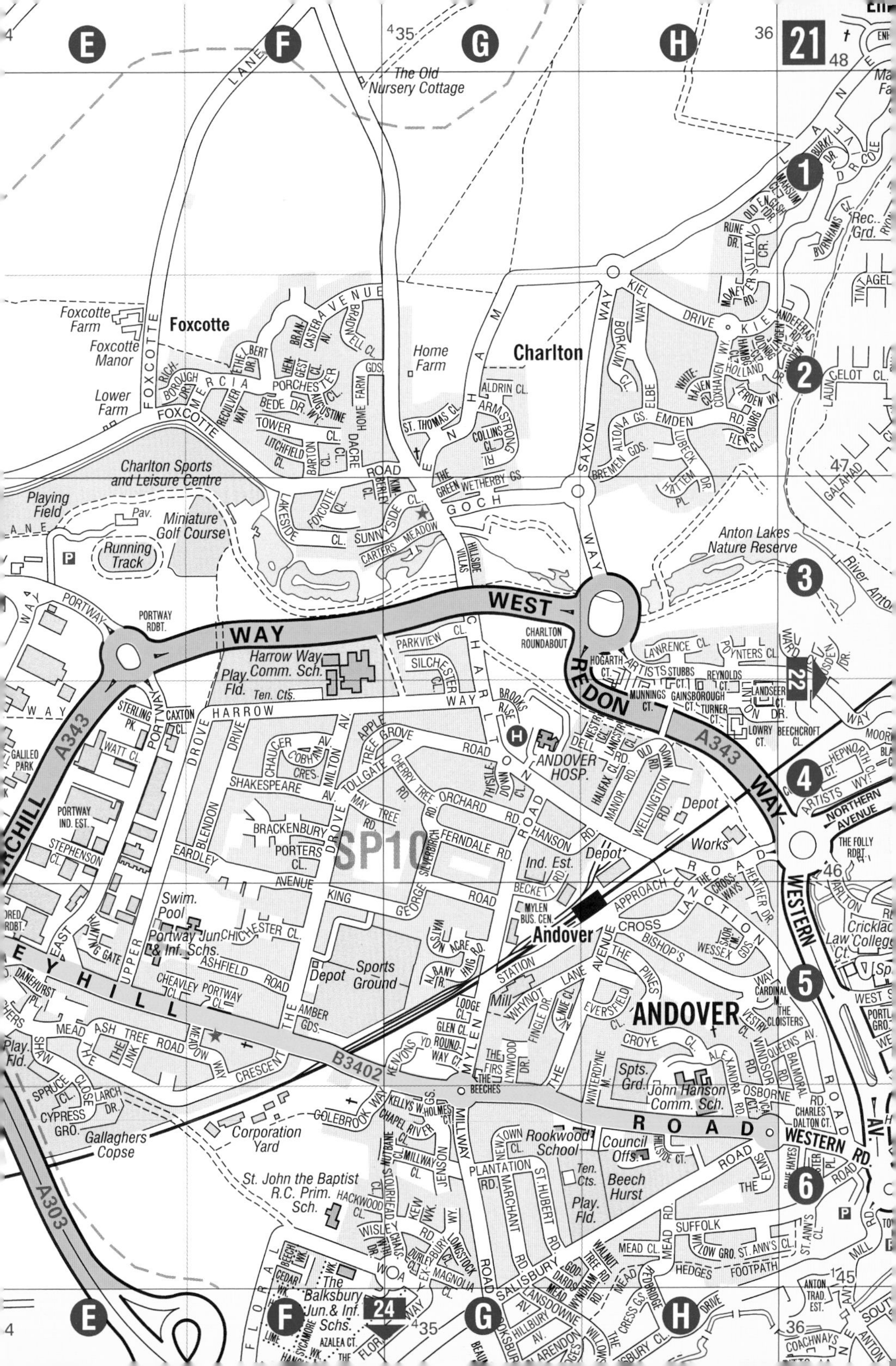

21
E
F
G
H
1
2
3
4
5
6
22
24
35
36
47
46
45
48
The Old Nursery Cottage
Foxcotte Farm
Foxcotte
Foxcotte Manor
Lower Farm
Home Farm
Charlton
Charlton Sports and Leisure Centre
Playing Field
Pav.
Miniature Golf Course
Running Track
Anton Lakes Nature Reserve
River Anton
WEST WAY
PORTWAY RDBT.
CHARLTON ROUNDABOUT
Harrow Way Comm. Sch.
Play. Fld.
Ten. Cts.
ANDOVER HOSP.
SP10
Depot
Works
Ind. Est.
MYLEN BUS. CEN.
Andover
ANDOVER
Swim. Pool
Portway Jun. & Inf. Schs.
Sports Ground
Mill
Spts. Grd.
John Hanson Comm. Sch.
Rookwood School
Council Offs.
Beech Hurst
Corporation Yard
Gallaghers Copse
St. John the Baptist R.C. Prim. Sch.
The Balksbury Jun. & Inf. Schs.
PORTWAY IND. EST.
GALILEO PARK
STERLING PK.
THE FOLLY RDBT.
Cricklade Law College
ANTON TRAD. EST.
A343
A303
B3402
FOXCOTTE
MERCIA
GOCH
SAXON WAY
REDON WAY
KIEL DRIVE
HARROW WAY
CHARLTON ROAD
JUNCTION ROAD
WESTERN ROAD
WEYHILL ROAD
NORTHERN AVENUE
ARTISTS WY.
SALISBURY RD.
MILLWAY ROAD
LANSDOWNE AV.
STATION APPROACH
CROSS LANE
SHAKESPEARE AV.
EARDLEY AVENUE
KING GEORGE ROAD
ORCHARD RD.
FERNDALE RD.
HANSON RD.
EMDEN RD.
LAUNCELOT CL.
GALAHAD
TINTAGEL

22
Knights Enham
East Anton
ANDOVER
SP10
Anton Lakes Nature Reserve
River Anton
NEWBURY ROAD
A343
NEW ST.
CHURCHILL WAY
A3093
NORTHERN AV.
A3057
WESTERN AV.
EASTERN AV.
WINCHESTER RD.
REDON WY.
WEYHILL RD.
WESTERN RD.
ENHAM LANE
SMANNELL WAY
RIVER WAY
PILGRIMS WAY
WALWORTH RD.
VIGO ROAD
CORUNNA MAIN
LONDON RD.
MICHELDEVER ROAD
LADIES WALK
ENHAM ARCH ROUNDABOUT
THE FOLLY RDBT.
SMANNELL RD. RDBT.
KING ARTHUR'S WAY RDBT.
KNIGHTS ENHAM RDBT.
BLACKSMITHS RDBT.
WALWORTH RDBT.
VIGO RD. RDBT.
TOWN STA. RDBT.
THE LAMB RDBT.
Manor Farm
Eastanton Farm Cottages
Eastanton Farm
Eastanton Manor Farm
Red Cottages
Rec. Grd.
Jun. & Inf. Schs.
Prim. Sch.
Shepherds Spring Jun. & Inf. Schs.
Playground
Factory
Works
Saw Mill
WESTMARCH BUS. CEN.
Icknield Sch.
Sub.
Depot
Wks.
Cemy.
War Mem.
Cricklade College
Law Ct.
Spts. Cen.
THE CHANTRY CEN.
Mus.
Bowl. Grn.
Ten. Cts.
Sports Centre
Pav.
Norman Gate School Playing Fields
The Mark Way Sch.
Winton School
Vigo Jun. & Inf. Schs.
Playgrd.
Prim. Sch.
H.P.O.
T.H.
Wolverdene School
Iron Bridge
Reservoirs (covered)
ANTON TRAD. EST.
John Hanson Comm. Sch.
Playing
A
B
C
D
1
2
3
4
5
6
36
37
45
46
47
48
21
25

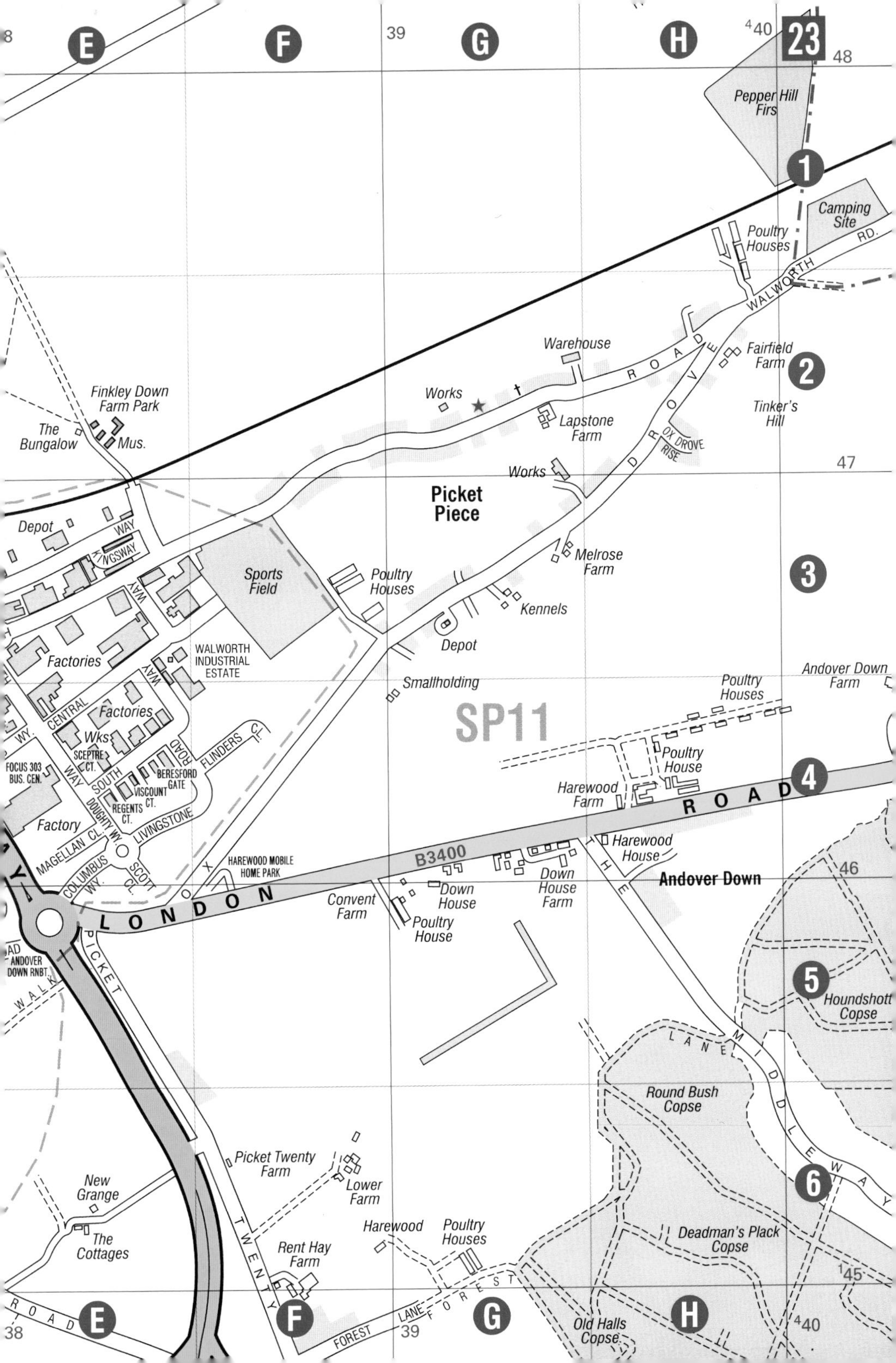
E
F
G
H
39
440
48
Pepper Hill Firs
1
Camping Site
Poultry Houses
WALWORTH RD.
Warehouse
ROAD
Fairfield Farm
2
Works
Lapstone Farm
DROVE
Tinker's Hill
OX DROVE RISE
Finkley Down Farm Park
The Bungalow
Mus.
Works
47
Picket Piece
Depot
WAY
KINGSWAY
Sports Field
Poultry Houses
Melrose Farm
3
Kennels
WAY
Factories
WALWORTH INDUSTRIAL ESTATE
Depot
WAY
Smallholding
Andover Down Farm
CENTRAL
Factories
Poultry Houses
SP11
WY.
Wks.
SCEPTRE CT.
FLINDERS CL.
ROAD
Poultry House
FOCUS 303 BUS. CEN.
WAY
SOUTH
BERESFORD GATE
4
VISCOUNT CT.
Harewood Farm
ROAD
REGENTS CT.
DOUGHTY WY.
Factory
LIVINGSTONE
MAGELLAN CL.
Harewood House
B3400
COLUMBUS WY.
SCOTT CL.
HAREWOOD MOBILE HOME PARK
OX
Down House Farm
Andover Down
46
Convent Farm
Down House
THE
LONDON
Poultry House
AD
ANDOVER DOWN RNBT.
PICKET
WALK
5
Houndshott Copse
LANE
MIDDLE
Round Bush Copse
WAY
Picket Twenty Farm
New Grange
Lower Farm
6
The Cottages
Harewood
Poultry Houses
Deadman's Plack Copse
TWENTY
Rent Hay Farm
FOREST
145
ROAD
LANE
Old Halls Copse
FOREST
38
39
440

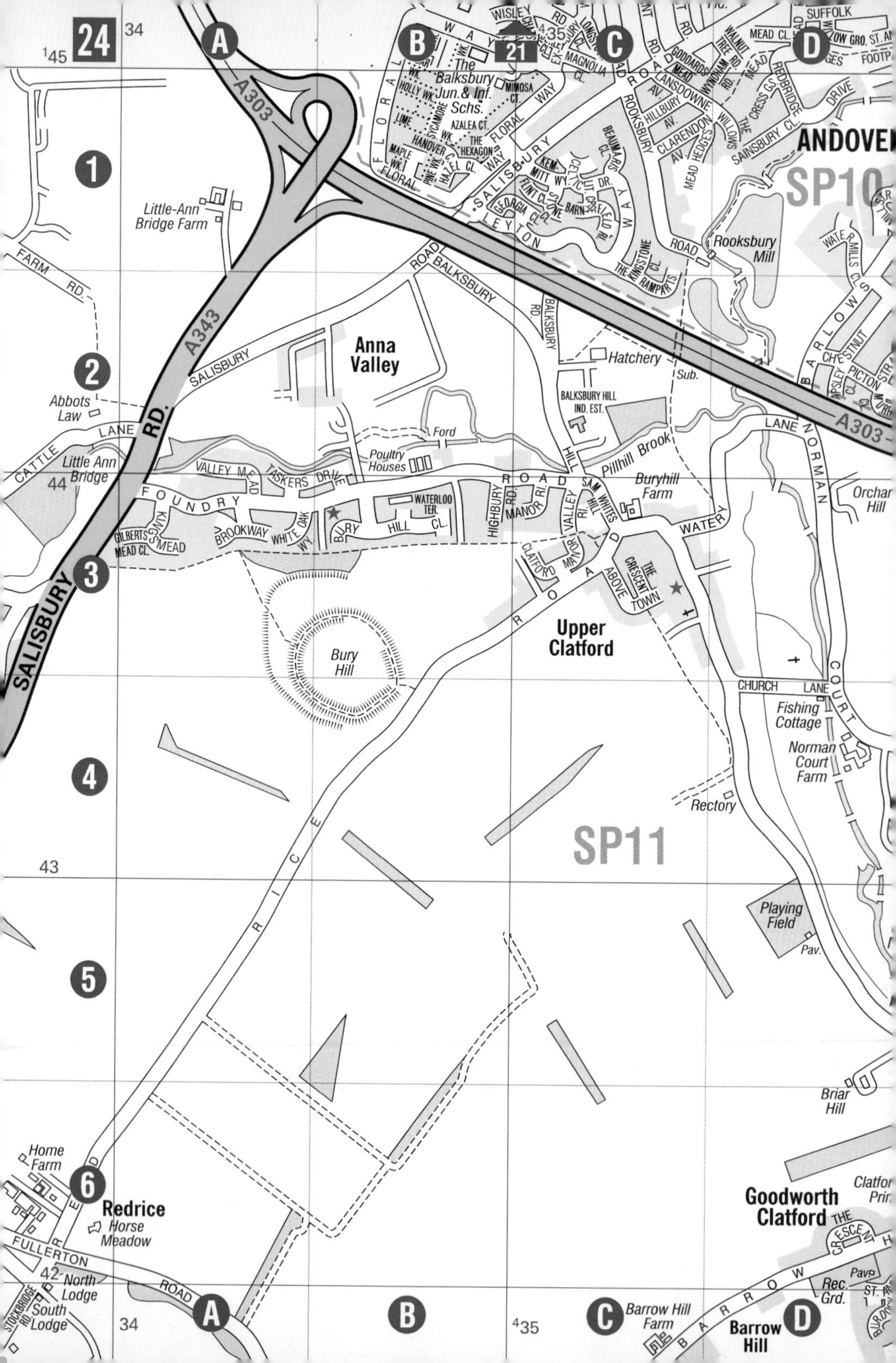

A303
A343
SALISBURY RD.
Little-Ann Bridge Farm
FARM RD.
Abbots Law
CATTLE LANE
Little Ann Bridge
Anna Valley
SALISBURY
BALKSBURY ROAD
BALKSBURY RD.
The Balksbury Jun.& Inf. Schs.
FLORAL WAY
HOLLY WK.
LIME WK.
SYCAMORE WK.
AZALEA CT.
MIMOSA CT.
THE HEXAGON
HANOVER CL.
MAPLE WK.
PINE WK.
HAZEL CL.
MAGNOLIA CL.
SALISBURY WAY
LEYTON WAY
GEORGIA CL.
FLINT CL.
KEMMITT WY.
CELTIC DR.
LIT. CORNFIELD RI.
BEAUMARIS CL.
ROOKSBURY ROAD
HILLBURY AV.
CLARENDON AV.
LANSDOWNE AV.
MEAD HEDGES
WILLOWS
GODDARDS MEAD
WYNDHAM RD.
WALNUT TREE RD.
THE CRESS GS.
REDBRIDGE DRIVE
SAINSBURY CL.
SUFFOLK
MEAD CL.
WILLOW GRO.
THE KINGSTONE CL.
THE RAMPARTS
Rooksbury Mill
ANDOVER
SP10
BARLOWS
CHESTNUT
PICTON
APSLEY CL.
WATER MILLS CL.
Hatchery
Sub.
BALKSBURY HILL IND. EST.
Ford
Poultry Houses
Pillhill Brook
Buryhill Farm
VALLEY MEAD
TASKERS DRIVE
FOUNDRY ROAD
WATERLOO TER.
BURY HILL CL.
HIGHBURY RD.
MANOR RI.
VALLEY RI.
SAM WHITES HILL
GILBERTS MEAD CL.
KINGS MEAD
BROOKWAY
WHITE OAK WY.
CLATFORD MANOR
THE CRESCENT
ABOVE TOWN
Upper Clatford
WATERY LANE
NORMAN COURT LANE
Orchard Hill
Bury Hill
CHURCH LANE
Fishing Cottage
Norman Court Farm
Rectory
SP11
Playing Field
Pav.
Briar Hill
REDRICE ROAD
Home Farm
Redrice
Horse Meadow
FULLERTON ROAD
North Lodge
South Lodge
STOCKBRIDGE RD.
Barrow Hill Farm
BARROW HILL
Barrow Hill
Goodworth Clatford
THE CRESCENT
Rec. Grd.
Pav.
21

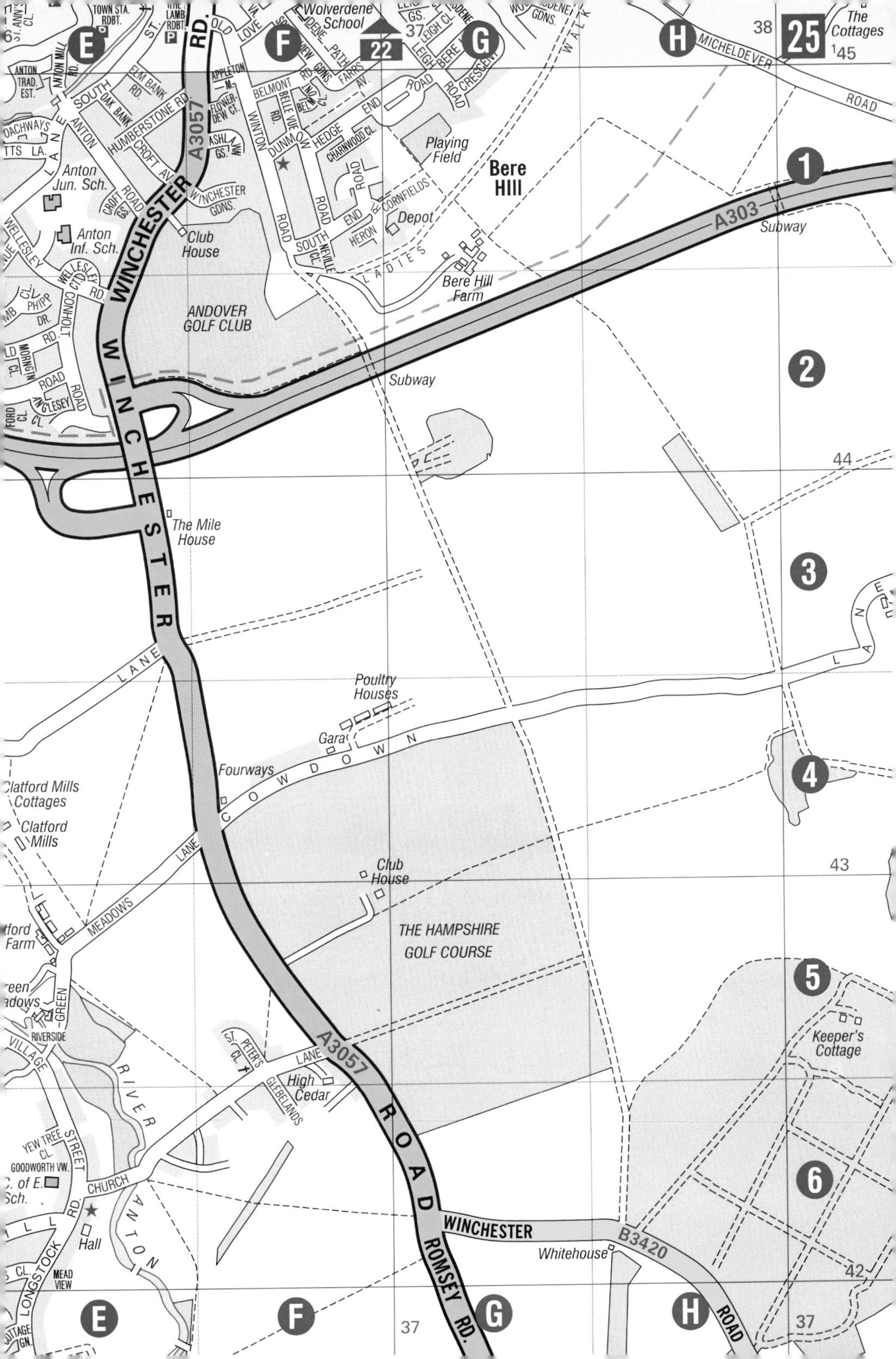
Wolverdene School
22
The Cottages
MICHELDEVER ROAD
WINCHESTER RD.
A3057
Playing Field
Bere Hill
Anton Jun. Sch.
Anton Inf. Sch.
Club House
Depot
LADIES WALK
Bere Hill Farm
A303
Subway
ANDOVER GOLF CLUB
The Mile House
Poultry Houses
Fourways
COWDOWN LANE
Clatford Mills Cottages
Clatford Mills
MEADOWS LANE
THE HAMPSHIRE GOLF COURSE
Keeper's Cottage
High Cedar
GLEBELANDS
RIVER ANTON
CHURCH LANE
Hall
WINCHESTER ROAD
B3420
Whitehouse
ROMSEY RD.
VILLAGE STREET
RIVERSIDE
YEW TREE CL.
GOODWORTH VW.
MEAD VIEW
LONGSTOCK
ST. PETER'S CL.
ANTON TRAD. EST.
HUMBERSTONE RD.
CROFT AV.
WINCHESTER GDNS.
SOUTH END
HEDGE END
CHARNWOOD CL.
CORNFIELDS
HERON
WINTON ROAD
DUNMOW
BELMONT
BELLE VUE RD.
APPLETON M.
FLOWERDEW CT.
ELM BANK RD.
OAK BANK
ANGLESEY
WELLESLEY
CONHOLT RD.
PHIPP
TOWN STA. RDBT.
THE LAMB RDBT.
A B C D E F G H
1 2 3 4 5 6
37 38 42 43 44 45

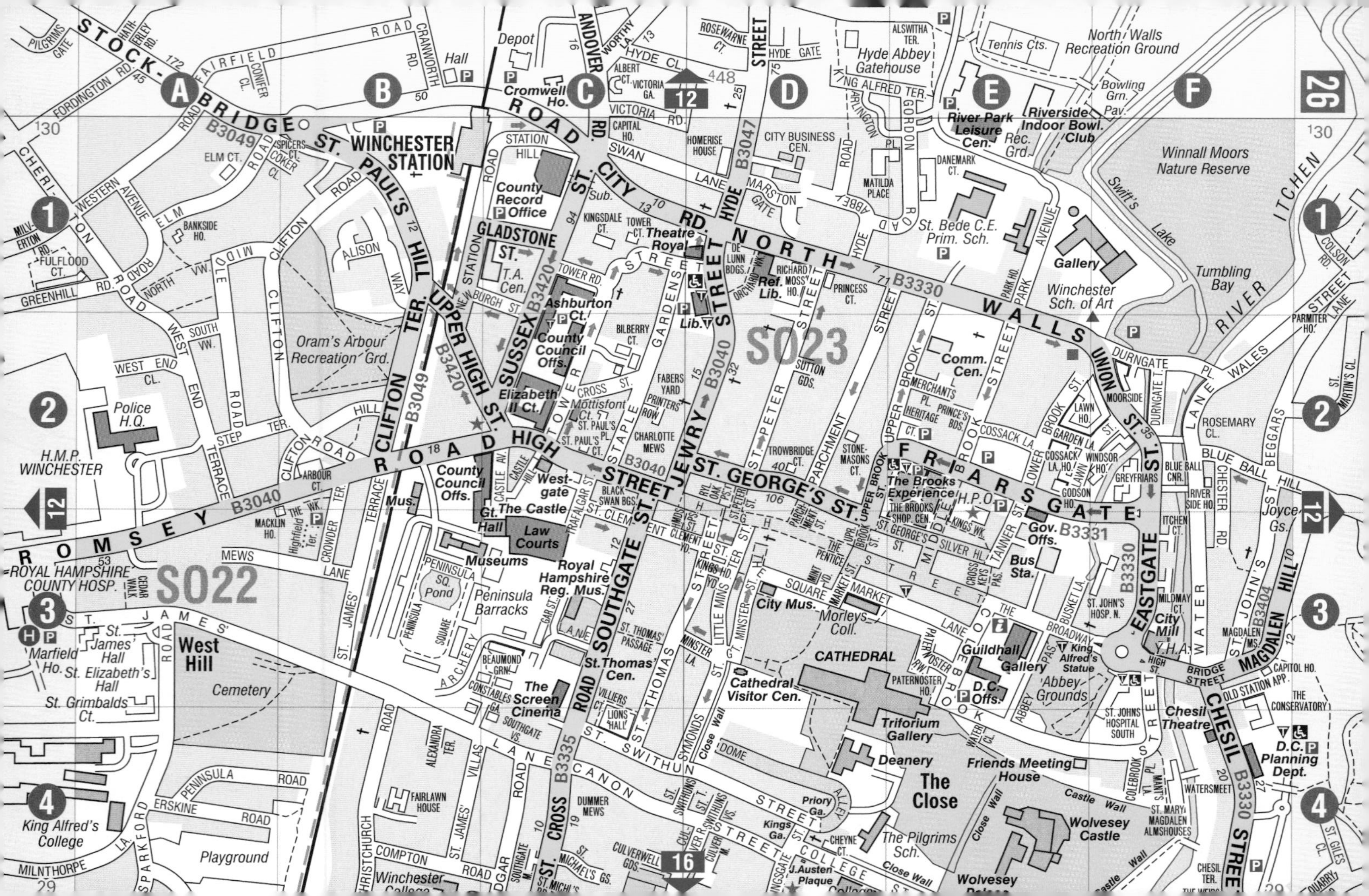

STOCKBRIDGE ROAD
Winchester Station
ST. PAUL'S HILL
Cromwell Ho.
ANDOVER RD.
CITY RD.
HYDE STREET
Hyde Abbey Gatehouse
North Walls Recreation Ground
Tennis Cts.
River Park Leisure Cen.
Riverside Indoor Bowl. Club
Winnall Moors Nature Reserve
Swift's Lake
Tumbling Bay
RIVER ITCHEN
Gallery
Winchester Sch. of Art
St. Bede C.E. Prim. Sch.
NORTH WALLS
UNION ST.
County Record Office
GLADSTONE ST.
Theatre Royal
Ref. Lib.
SO23
Comm. Cen.
Ashburton Ct.
County Council Offs.
Elizabeth II Ct.
UPPER HIGH ST.
CLIFTON TER.
Oram's Arbour Recreation Grd.
Police H.Q.
H.M.P. WINCHESTER
ROMSEY ROAD
ROYAL HAMPSHIRE COUNTY HOSP.
SO22
HIGH STREET
JEWRY ST.
ST. GEORGE'S ST.
FRIARSGATE
EASTGATE ST.
The Brooks Experience
Gov. Offs.
Bus Sta.
Westgate
The Castle
Gt. Hall
Law Courts
Museums
Royal Hampshire Reg. Mus.
Peninsula Barracks
SOUTHGATE ROAD
City Mus.
Morleys Coll.
CATHEDRAL
Cathedral Visitor Cen.
Guildhall Gallery
D.C. Offs.
King Alfred's Statue
Abbey Grounds
City Mill
MAGDALEN HILL
CHESIL STREET
Chesil Theatre
D.C. Planning Dept.
St. Thomas' Cen.
The Screen Cinema
Triforium Gallery
Deanery
The Close
Friends Meeting House
Wolvesey Castle
The Pilgrims Sch.
West Hill Cemetery
St. James' Hall
St. Elizabeth's Hall
St. Grimbalds Ct.
King Alfred's College
Playground
ST. CROSS ROAD
CANON STREET
ST. SWITHUN STREET
COLLEGE STREET
J.Austen Plaque
Winchester College

INDEX

Including Streets, Places & Areas, Industrial Estates, Selected Subsidiary Addresses and Selected Places of Interest.

HOW TO USE THIS INDEX

1. Each street name is followed by its Posttown or Postal Locality and then by its map reference; e.g. Abbey Hill Rd. *Win* —3B **12** is in the Winchester Posttown and is to be found in square 3B on page **12**. The page number being shown in bold type.
   A strict alphabetical order is followed in which Av., Rd., St., etc. (though abbreviated) are read in full and as part of the street name; e.g. Ashurst Clo. appears after Ash Tree Rd. but before Ash Wlk.

2. Streets and a selection of Subsidiary names not shown on the Maps, appear in the index in *Italics* with the thoroughfare to which it is connected shown in brackets; e.g. *Alton Ct. Win —3C **12** (off Northlands Dri.)*

3. Places and areas are shown in the index in **bold type**, the map reference referring to the actual map square in which the town or area is located and not to the place name; e.g. **Andover.—5H 21**

4. An example of a selected place of interest is Andover Golf Club. —1E 25

5. Map references shown in brackets; e.g. Abbey Pas. *Win* —6C **12** (4E **26**) refer to entries that also appear on the large scale page **26**.

GENERAL ABBREVIATIONS

All : Alley
App : Approach
Arc : Arcade
Av : Avenue
Bk : Back
Boulevd : Boulevard
Bri : Bridge
B'way : Broadway
Bldgs : Buildings
Bus : Business
Cvn : Caravan
Cen : Centre
Chu : Church
Chyd : Churchyard
Circ : Circle
Cir : Circus
Clo : Close
Comn : Common
Cotts : Cottages
Ct : Court
Cres : Crescent
Cft : Croft
Dri : Drive
E : East
Embkmt : Embankment
Est : Estate
Fld : Field
Gdns : Gardens
Gth : Garth
Ga : Gate
Gt : Great
Grn : Green
Gro : Grove
Ho : House
Ind : Industrial
Info : Information
Junct : Junction
La : Lane
Lit : Little
Lwr : Lower
Mc : Mac
Mnr : Manor
Mans : Mansions
Mkt : Market
Mdw : Meadow
M : Mews
Mt : Mount
Mus : Museum
N : North
Pal : Palace
Pde : Parade
Pk : Park
Pas : Passage
Pl : Place
Quad : Quadrant
Res : Residential
Ri : Rise
Rd : Road
Shop : Shopping
S : South
Sq : Square
Sta : Station
St : Street
Ter : Terrace
Trad : Trading
Up : Upper
Va : Vale
Vw : View
Vs : Villas
Vis : Visitors
Wlk : Walk
W : West
Yd : Yard

POSTTOWN AND POSTAL LOCALITY ABBREVIATIONS

Abb W : Abbots Worthy
Abb A : Abbotts Ann
Alr : Alresford
And : Andover
And D : Andover Down
Anna V : Anna Valley
Avtn : Avington
Bish S : Bishops Sutton
Bram : Brambridge
Charl : Charlton
Chilc : Chilcomb
Cla : Clanville
Col C : Colden Common
Comp : Compton
Cot : Cottonworth
Estn : Easton
Fobd : Fobdown
Good C : Goodworth Clatford
Highb : Highbridge
Hurs : Hursley
It Ab : Itchen Abbas
It Sto : Itchen Stoke
King W : Kings Worthy
L Pk : Little Park
Longp : Longparish
Mart W : Martyr Worthy
More : Morestead
Old Al : Old Alresford
Ott : Otterbourne
P Cnr : Penton Corner
Pen G : Penton Grafton
Pen H : Penton Harroway
Pen M : Penton Mewsey
Pic P : Picket Piece
P Twen : Picket Twenty
Red P : Red Post Bridge
Shaw : Shaw
Sman : Smannell
S Won : South Wonston
Spar : Sparsholt
Twy : Twyford
Up Cl : Upper Clatford
Wal I : Walworth Ind. Est.
W'hll : Weyhill
Wher : Wherwell
Win : Winchester
Wor D : Worthy Down

INDEX

Abbey Hill Clo. *Win* —3C **12**
Abbey Hill Rd. *Win* —3B **12**
Abbey Pas. *Win* —6C **12** (4E **26**)
Abbotstone Rd. *Fobd* —1C **8**
Abbots Worthy. —5F 5
Abbotts Ann Rd. *Win* —2H **11**
Abbotts Clo. *Win* —3C **12**
Abbotts Ct. *Win* —3B **12**
Abbotts Rd. *Win* —3C **12**
Above Town. *Up Cl* —3C **24**
Acorn Clo. *Win* —3H **11**
Acre Ct. *And* —5B **22**
Acre Path. *And* —5B **22**
Addison Clo. *Win* —2G **15**
Adelaide Rd. *And* —5B **22**
Admirals Way. *And* —5D **22**
Agricola Wlk. *And* —2B **22**
Airlie Corner. *Win* —1A **16**
Airlie Rd. *Win* —1A **16**
Albany Rd. *And* —5G **21**
Albert Ct. *Win* —4B **12** (1C **26**)
Alders Ct. *Alr* —3F **9**
Aldrin Clo. *Charl* —2G **21**
Alexander Bell Cen. *And* —4D **20**
Alexandra Rd. *And* —5H **21**
Alexandra Ter. *Win* —6B **12** (4B **26**)
Alison Way. *Win* —5B **12** (1B **26**)
Alresford Golf Course. —6E 9
Alresford Rd. *Win* —6D **12** (2F **26**)
Alswitha Ter. *Win* —4C **12** (1E **26**)
Altona Gdns. *And* —2H **21**
*Alton Ct. Win —3C **12***
(off Northlands Dri.)
Amber Gdns. *And* —5F **21**
Amport Clo. *Win* —2G **11**
Andeferas Rd. *And* —2A **22**
Anders Rd. *S Won* —1D **2**
Andover. —5H 21
Andover Down. —4H 23
Andover Down Roundabout. *And* —5E **23**
Andover Golf Club. —2F 25
Andover Mus. —5B 22
Andover Rd. *Win* —2A **12** (1C **26**)
Andover Rd. N. *Win* —6H **3**
Andover Rd. Retail Pk. *Win* —4B **12**
Anglesey Clo. *And* —2E **25**
Anna Valley. —3B 24
Anton Mill Rd. *And* —1E **25**
Anton Rd. *And* —1E **25**
Anton Trad. Est. *And* —6A **22**
Appledown Clo. *Alr* —5F **9**
Appledown La. *Alr* —6G **9**
Appleshaw Clo. *Win* —1H **11**
Appleton M. *And* —1F **25**
Apple Tree Gro. *And* —4F **21**
Apsley Clo. *And* —2D **24**
Arbour Ct. *Win* —2B **26**
Archery La. *Win* —6B **12** (3B **26**)
Arkwright Ga. *And* —3D **20**
Arlebury Pk. *Alr* —3D **8**
Arle Clo. *Alr* —3E **9**
Arle Gdns. *Alr* —3F **9**
Arlington Pl. *Win* —1D **26**
Armstrong Clo. *S Won* —1D **2**
Armstrong Ri. *Charl* —2G **21**
Arthur Rd. *Win* —4C **12**
Artists Way. *And* —3H **21**
Arundel Clo. *Alr* —5E **9**
Ashbarn Cres. *Win* —2H **15**
Ashburton Clo. *Alr* —4E **9**
Ashburton Rd. *Alr* —4E **9**
Ashfield Rd. *And* —5F **21**
Ashlawn Gdns. *And* —1F **25**
Ashley Clo. *Win* —2G **11**
Ashmore Rd. *Win* —4G **11**
Ash Tree Rd. *And* —5E **21**
Ashurst Clo. *Win* —2H **11**
Ash Wlk. *Alr* —4F **9**
Atholl Ct. *And* —2A **22**
Attwoods Drove. *Comp* —1C **18**
Augustine Way. *Charl* —2F **21**
Augustus Wlk. *And* —2B **22**
Austen Av. *Win* —3F **15**
Austen Clo. *Win* —3C **12**
Avenue Clo. *And* —5G **21**
Avenue Rd. *Win* —5A **12** (1A **26**)
Avenue, The. *Alr* —4D **8**
Avenue, The. *And* —5G **21**
Avenue, The. *Twy* —3G **19**
Avington Pk. —6E 7
Avlan Ct. *Win* —2B **16**
Avon Ct. *And* —3C **22**
Azalea Ct. *And* —1B **24**

Back St. *Win* —3B **16**
Badger Farm. —3G 15
Badger Farm Rd. *Win* —2F **15**
(in two parts)
Baigent Clo. *Win* —5E **13**
Bailey Clo. *Win* —1H **15**
Balksbury Hill. *Up Cl* —1B **24**
Balksbury Hill Ind. Est. *Up Cl* —2C **24**
Balksbury Rd. *Up Cl* —2C **24**
Balmoral Rd. *And* —5A **22**
Bankside Ho. *Win* —5A **12** (1A **26**)
Barcelona Clo. *And* —4B **22**
Bar End Ind. Est. *Win* —2D **16**
Bar End Rd. *Win* —1D **16**
(in two parts)
Barfield Clo. *Win* —1D **16**
Baring Clo. *It Ab* —4G **7**
Baring Rd. *Win* —6D **12**
Barley Down Dri. *Win* —3H **15**
Barlows La. *And* —2D **24**

Barnes Clo. Win —2A 16
Barnfield Ri. And —1C 24
Barrow Hill. —6D 24
Barrow Hill. Good C —6C 24
Bartholomew Clo. Win —4C 12
Barton Clo. Charl —2F 21
Basingstoke Rd. King W & Abb W —5F 5
Basingstoke Rd. Old Al —1F 9
Batchelor's Barn Rd. And —5C 22
Battery Hill. Win —1G 15
Beales Clo. And —5B 22
Beatty Ct. And —5D 22
Beaufort Rd. Win —1B 16
Beaulieu Clo. Win —1H 11
Beaumaris Clo. And —1C 24
Beaumond Grn. Win —3C 26
Beckett Rd. And —5G 21
Bede Dri. Charl —2F 21
Bedfield La. Win —6D 4
Bedser Sq. And —2B 22
Beech Clo. P Cnr —4C 20
Beech Clo. Win —4F 15
Beech Copse. Win —4F 11
Beechcroft Clo. And —4A 22
Beeches, The. And —5G 21
Beech Rd. Alr —4F 9
Beech Wlk. And —6F 21
Beggars La. Win —5D 12 (2F 26)
Bellevue Rd. And —1F 25
Bell Ho. Alr —5F 9
Bell Rd. And —5C 22
Belmont Clo. And —1F 25
Belmont Rd. And —1F 25
Benbow Ct. And —5D 22
Benenden Grn. Alr —5F 9
Bentley Clo. King W —5D 4
Bercote Clo. Win —6F 3
Bere Clo. Win —3H 11
Bere Hill. —1F 25
Bere Hill Cres. And —6C 22
Beresford Clo. And —2E 25
Beresford Ga. And —4E 23
Bereweeke Av. Win —2A 12
Bereweeke Clo. Win —4A 12
Bereweeke Rd. Win —4A 12
Bereweeke Way. Win —3A 12
Berry La. Twy —2F 19
Beyne Rd. Win —4F 15
Bilbao Ct. And —4D 22
Bilberry Ct. Win —5B 12 (2C 26)
Birch Ct. Win —1G 15
Birinus Rd. Win —4C 12
Bishops Sutton Rd. Alr —3G 9
Bishop's Way. And —5H 21
Blackbird Ct. And —2B 22
Blacksmiths Roundabout. And —4B 22
Black Swan Bldgs. Win —2C 26
Black Swan Yd. And —5B 22
Blackthorn Clo. S Won —1B 2
Blackwell Rd. Wor D —2B 2
Blakes Ct. And —4A 22
Blendon Dri. And —4F 21
Blue Ball Corner. Win —2F 26
Blue Ball Hill. Win —5D 12 (2F 26)
Blue Hayes Clo. And —6A 22
Borden Gates. And —6A 22
Borkum Clo. And —2H 21
Borman Way. S Won —1D 2
Borsberry Clo. And —5B 22
Boscobel Rd. Win —4B 12
Boscowen Clo. And —5D 22 (off London Rd.)
Bostock Clo. Spar —2B 10
Bourne Clo. Ott —5C 18
Bourne Ct. And —3C 22 (off River Way)
Bournefields. Twy —2H 19
Bourne La. Twy —2G 19
Boyne Mead Rd. King W —4D 4
Boyne Ri. King W —3D 4
Bracher Clo. And —5B 22
Brackenbury. And —4F 21
Bradley Peak. Win —4G 11
Bradley Rd. Win —2G 11
Bradman Sq. And —2B 22 (off Cricketers Way)
Bradwell Clo. Charl —2F 21
Braeside Clo. Win —3F 15
Bramble Hill. Alr —4F 9
Bramshaw Clo. Win —2G 11
Brancaster Av. Charl —2F 21
Brandy Mt. Alr —3F 9
Branksome Clo. Win —1F 15
Brassey Rd. Win —4B 12
Braxton Ho. Win —4E 13
Bremen Gdns. And —2H 21
Brewers La. Twy —4F 19
Bridge Rd. Alr —4D 8
Bridge St. And —6A 22
Bridge St. Win —6D 12 (3F 26)
Bridge Ter. Shaw —3E 19
Bridgetts La. Mart W —1H 5
Broad Chalke Down. Win —3G 15
Broad St. Alr —3F 9
Broad Vw. La. Win —4E 15
Broadway, The. And —6A 22 (off Western Rd.)
Broadway, The. Win —6C 12 (3E 26)
Brooke Clo. King W —3D 4
Brooklyn Clo. Ott —6C 18
Brooks Experience, The. —2E 26
Brooks Ri. And —4G 21
Brooks Shop. Cen., The. Win —5C 12 (2E 26)
Brook, The. Old Al —1F 9
Brookway. Anna V —3A 24
Browning Dri. Win —5H 11
Brunel Ga. And —3D 20
Burdock Clo. Good C —6D 24
Buriton Rd. Win —1H 11
Burkal Dri. And —1A 22
Burley Rd. Win —1H 11
Burne Clo. Wor D —1H 3
Burnett Clo. Win —3G 11
Burnhams Clo. And —1A 22
Burns Clo. S Won —1D 2
Burrow Rd. Spar —5A 10
Bury Hill Clo. Anna V —3B 24
Busket La. Win —6C 12 (3E 26)
Buttermere Gdns. Alr —5F 9
Butts Clo. Win —4H 11
Byng Wlk. And —5D 22
Byron Av. Win —5H 11

Caerleon Dri. And —1A 22
Caesar Rd. And —2B 22
Calder Ct. And —3C 22
Camelot Clo. And —3A 22
Campion Way. King W —5E 5
Canon St. Win —6B 12 (4C 26)
Canute Rd. Win —1D 16
Capital Ho. Win —1C 26
Cardinal M. And —5H 21
Carisbrooke Clo. Alr —5F 9
Carmans La. Comp —1D 18
Carpenters. Alr —4F 9
Carters Mdw. Charl —3F 21
Castle Av. Win —5B 12 (2C 26)
Castle Hill. Win —5B 12 (2C 26)
Castle Ri. King W —2E 5
Cathedral Vw. Win —1D 16
Cattle La. Abb A —2A 24
Cavendish Gro. Win —2D 12
Caxton Clo. And —4E 21
Cedar Clo. King W —3D 4
Cedar Wlk. And —6F 21
Cedar Wlk. Win —6A 12 (3A 26)
Cedarwood. King W —4E 5
Celtic Dri. And —1C 24
Central Way. And —4E 23
Chalkcroft La. Pen M —2C 20
Chalk Ridge. Win —6E 13
Chantry Cen., The. And —5A 22
Chantry St. And —5A 22
Chapel La. Estn & Win —6A 6 & 1H 13
Chapelriver Clo. And —6G 21
Charfield Clo. Win —2A 16
Charles Clo. Win —3D 12
Charles Dalton Ct. And —6A 22
Charlotte Clo. And —5D 22
Charlotte M. Win —2C 26
Charlton. —2G 21
Charlton Rd. And —3G 21
Charlton Roundabout. And —3G 21
Charnwood Clo. And —1F 25
Chatham Rd. Win —2G 15
Chatsworth Dri. And —6G 21
Chaucer Av. And —4F 21
Chaucer Clo. S Won —1D 2
Chaundler Rd. Win —3C 12
Chawton Clo. Win —1H 11
Cheavley Clo. And —5E 21
Cheriton Clo. Win —4H 11
Cheriton Rd. Win —4H 11 (1A 26)
Cherry Clo. S Won —1C 2
Cherry Tree Rd. And —4G 21
Chesil St. Win —6D 12 (4F 26)
Chesil Ter. Win —6D 12 (4F 26)
Chester Rd. Win —5D 12 (2F 26)
Chestnut Av. And —2D 24
Chestnut Av. Win —1F 11
Chestnut Mead. Win —2B 16
Chestnut Wlk. Alr —4F 9
Cheyne Ct. Win —4D 26
Chichester Clo. And —5F 21
Chilbolton Av. Win —5H 11
Chilbolton Ct. Win —6G 11
Chilcomb. —3H 17
Chilcombe Heights. Win —6D 12 (off Quarry Rd.)
Chilcomb La. Win & Chilc —2D 16 (in two parts)
Chillandham La. It Ab —1C 6
Chilland La. Mart W —5C 6
Chiltern Ct. Alr —4F 9
Christchurch Gdns. Win —2B 16
Christchurch Rd. Win —2A 16 (in two parts)
Christmas Hill. S Won —1A 2
Church Clo. And —5B 22 (off East St.)
Churchfields. Twy —3G 19
Churchfields Rd. Twy —3F 19
Churchill Clo. King W —2D 4
Churchill Way. And —4B 22
Churchill Way W. And —4E 21
Church La. Estn —6H 5
Church La. Good C —6E 25
Church La. King W —5E 5
Church La. Mart W —5B 6
Church La. Spar —2A 10
Church La. Twy —2G 19
Church La. Up Cl —4D 24
Church La. Win —5E 3
Churchyard Cotts. Alr —3F 9
City Bus. Cen. Win —5C 12 (1D 26)
City Mus. —6C 12 (3D 26)
City Rd. Win —5B 12 (1C 26)
Clarendon Av. And —1C 24
Clatford Mnr. Up Cl —3C 24
Claudius Clo. And —1B 22
Clausentum Rd. Win —2B 16
Clease Way. Comp —2C 18
Cliff Way. Comp —3D 18
Clifton Hill. Win —5B 12 (2B 26)
Clifton Rd. Win —5A 12 (1A 26)
Clifton Ter. Win —5B 12 (2B 26)
Cloisters, The. And —5A 22
Cloverbank. King W —1D 4
Clyde Ct. And —3C 22
Coachways. And —1E 25
Coate Dri. Wor D —1G 3
Cobbett Clo. Win —2G 15
Coker Clo. Win —5B 12 (1A 26)
Colbourne Ct. Win —3C 12
Colden La. Old Al —1G 9
Colebrook Pl. Win —6D 12 (4F 26)
Colebrook St. Win —6C 12 (3E 26)
Colebrook Way. And —6F 21
Cole Clo. And —1A 22
Colenzo Dri. And —4B 22
Coles Clo. Twy —2G 19
Coles Mede. Ott —6B 18 (in two parts)
College St. Win —6C 12 (4D 26)
College Wlk. Win —1C 16
Colley Clo. Win —2C 12
Collingwood Wlk. And —5D 22
Collins Clo. Charl —2G 21
Colson Clo. Win —5D 12 (1F 26)
Colson Rd. Win —5D 12 (1F 26)
Columbus Way. And —4E 23
Compton. —1D 18
Compton Clo. Win —4F 15
Compton Rd. Win —6B 12 (4B 26)
Compton Sq. And —2C 22
Compton St. Comp —1C 18
Compton Way. Win —4F 15
Coney Grn. Win —3C 12
Conholt Rd. And —2E 25
Conifer Clo. Win —4A 12 (1A 26)
Coniston Gro. Alr —5F 9
Connaught Rd. Wor D —1G 3 (in two parts)
Conservatory, The. Win —6D 12 (3F 26)
Constable Ct. And —4A 22
Constables Ga. Win —3B 26
Constantine Sq. And —2C 22 (off Cricketers Way)
Coopers Clo. Wor D —1H 3
Coppice Clo. Win —4G 11
Copse Clo. Ott —5C 18
Coram Clo. Win —3C 12
Corfe Clo. Alr —5E 9
Corinthian Clo. And —1B 22
Cornerways. King W —5D 4
Cornes Clo. Win —6H 11
Cornfields. And —1G 25
Corunna Main. And —5B 22
Cossack La. Win —5C 12 (2E 26)
Cossack La. Ho. Win —2E 26
Couch Grn. Mart W —4C 6
Courtenay Rd. Win —3C 12
Court Rd. King W —6E 5
Coventry Ct. Win —3C 12
Covey Way. Alr —5D 8
Cowdown La. Good C —4F 25
Cowdrey Sq. And —2B 22
Cowley Dri. Wor D —1H 3
Cox's Hill. Twy —1G 19
Crab Wood Nature Reserve. —5B 10
Craddock Ho. Win —4E 13
Cranbourne Dri. Ott —6B 18
Cranbury Clo. Ott —6B 18
Cranworth Rd. Win —4B 12 (1B 26)
Crescent Clo. Win —3F 15
Crescent, The. And —5E 21
Crescent, The. Good C —6D 24
Crescent, The. Twy —3G 19
Crescent, The. Up Cl —3C 24
Cress Gdns. And —1D 24
Cricketers Way. And —2B 22
Cripstead La. Win —2B 16
Croft Av. And —1E 25
Croft Gdns. And —1E 25
Cromwell Rd. Win —2H 15
Cross Keys Pas. Win —3E 26
Cross La. And —5H 21
Cross St. Win —5B 12 (2C 26)
Crossways. Shaw —4D 18
Crossways, The. And —4H 21
Croucher's Cft. Win —3G 11
Crowder Ter. Win —6B 12 (3B 26)
Crown Way. And —4D 22
Croye Clo. And —5H 21
Culley Vw. Alr —5F 9
Culver M. Win —6C 12 (4D 26)
Culver Rd. Win —1B 16
Culverwell Gdns. Win —6B 12 (4C 26)
Cundell Way. King W —2D 4
Cusden Dri. And —3A 22
Cuxhaven Way. And —2H 21
Cypress Gro. And —6E 21

Dacre Clo. Charl —2F 21
Dale Clo. Win —6E 3
Dances Clo. And —4B 22
Danegeld Clo. And —1B 22
Danehurst Pl. And —5E 21
Danemark Ct. Win —5C 12 (1E 26)
Danes Rd. Win —4C 12
Dawn Gdns. Win —1G 15
Dean. —2C 10
Dean Clo. Win —3G 11
Deane Down Drove. Win —1F 11
Deanery. —6C 12 (4D 26)
Dean La. Spar & Win —2B 10
Dean, The. Alr —3E 9
Dell Rd. And —4G 21
Dell Rd. Win —1E 17
De-Lucy Av. Alr —4D 8
De Lunn Bldgs. Win —1D 26
Dene Ct. And —6B 22
Dene Path. And —6B 22
Dene Rd. And —6B 22
Denham Clo. Win —3B 12
Denham Ct. Win —3C 12
Dennett Ho. Win —4F 13
Derwent Gdns. Alr —5F 9
Devenish Rd. Win —2H 11
Dexter Sq. And —2C 22
Dickenson Wlk. Alr —5F 9
Dickson Rd. And —6C 20
Dolphin Hill. Twy —3G 19
Dome All. Win —6C 12 (4D 26)
Domum Rd. Win —1D 16
Donnington Ct. Win —4C 12
Dorian Gro. Alr —5D 8
Doughty Way. And —4E 23
Douglas Rd. And —5D 20
Dove Clo. And —3B 22
Dover Clo. Alr —5F 9
Down Farm La. Win —3G 3
Down Ga. Alr —5E 9
Downlands Rd. Win —3F 15
Downlands Way. S Won —1B 2 (in two parts)
Downside Rd. Win —3F 11
Downs Rd. S Won —1B 2
Drake Ct. And —4D 22

Drayton St. *Win* —1G **15**
Drove Clo. *Twy* —4F **19**
Drove La. *Alr* —3C **8**
Drove, The. *And* —5F **21**
Drove, The. *Twy* —4F **19**
Drummond Clo. *Win* —2A **16**
Duke Clo. *And* —4D **22**
Dummer M. *Win* —6B **12** (4C **26**)
Duncan Ct. *And* —5D **22**
Dunmow Rd. *And* —1F **25**
Durley Clo. *And* —6G **21**
Durngate Pl. *Win* —5D **12** (2F **26**)
Durngate Ter. *Win* —5D **12** (2F **26**)
Dyson Dri. *Win* —3C **12**

Eardley Av. *And* —4E **21**
Earle Ho. *Win* —5F **13**
Eastacre. *Win* —4A **12**
East Anton. —1C 22
Eastern Av. *And* —6B **22**
Eastfield Clo. *And* —5C **22**
Eastfield Rd. *And* —5B **22**
Eastgate St. *Win* —6D **12** (3F **26**)
East Hill. *Win* —1D **16**
East La. *Alr* —5A **8**
Easton. —6A 6
Easton La. *Estn* —5A **6**
Easton La. *Win* —5D **12** (1F **26**)
Easton La. Bus. Cen. *Win* —5D **12**
East Portway. *And* —5E **21**
East St. *Alr* —3F **9**
East St. *And* —5B **22**
(in two parts)
E. Woodhay Rd. *Win* —1H **11**
Ebden Rd. *Win* —5D **12** (1F **26**)
Edgar Clo. *And* —1B **22**
Edgar Rd. *Win* —1B **16**
Edgar Vs. *Win* —6B **12**
Edinburgh Rd. *King W* —2D **4**
Edington Rd. *Win* —3C **12**
Edrich Sq. *And* —3B **22**
Edward Rd. *Win* —2A **16**
Edward Ter. *Alr* —4F **9**
Egbert Rd. *Win* —4C **12**
Elbe Way. *And* —2H **21**
Elder Clo. *Win* —3G **15**
Elder Ct. *Win* —3G **15**
Eling Clo. *Win* —2H **11**
Elizabeth Clo. *King W* —2D **4**
Ellingham Clo. *Alr* —4F **9**
Ellington Clo. *And* —6D **20**
Elm Bank Rd. *And* —1E **25**
Elm Ct. *Win* —5A **12** (1A **26**)
Elm Rd. *Alr* —4F **9**
Elm Rd. *Win* —5A **12** (1A **26**)
Elms, The. *And* —6H **21**
Emden Rd. *And* —2H **21**
Enham Arch Roundabout. *And* —3B **22**
Enham La. *And* —1A **22**
Enham La. *Charl* —2G **21**
Enmill La. *Win* —1A **14**
Ennerdale Gdns. *Alr* —5F **9**
Erasmus Pk. *Win* —4E **13**
Erskine Rd. *Win* —6A **12** (4A **26**)
Ethelbert Dri. *Charl* —2F **21**
Evelyn M. *Alr* —3F **9**
Eversfield Clo. *And* —5H **21**
Eversley Pl. *Win* —2H **15**
Exbury Way. *And* —6G **21**

Fabers Yd. *Win* —5B **12** (2C **26**)
Fairclose Dri. *Win* —6F **3**
Fairdown Clo. *Win* —6E **13**
Fairfax Clo. *Win* —2F **15**
Fairfield Rd. *Shaw* —4D **18**
Fairfield Rd. *Win* —4A **12** (1A **26**)
Fair La. *Win* —5H **13**
Fairlawn Ho. *Win* —6B **12** (4B **26**)
Fairview. *Alr* —5E **9**
Falcon Vw. *Win* —3G **15**
Fallow Fld. *Win* —3G **15**
Faraday Pk. *And* —4D **20**
Faringdon Ct. *Win* —3C **12**
Farley Clo. *Win* —3F **15**
Farley Mount Country Pk. —5A 10
Farley Mt. Rd. *Hurs* —4A **14**
Farm Rd. *L Pk* —1A **24**
Farrs Av. *And* —1F **25**
Fawley La. *More* —6H **17**
Felmer Dri. *King W* —4E **5**
Ferndale Rd. *And* —4G **21**
Field Clo. *Comp* —3C **18**
Field End. *King W* —4E **5**
Field Way. *Comp* —3C **18**
Finch's La. *Twy* —3F **19**
Fingle Dri. *And* —5G **21**
Finkley Down Farm Pk. & Mus. —2E 23
Fiona Clo. *Win* —5E **13**
Firmstone Rd. *Win* —5D **12**
Firs Cres. *King W* —3D **4**
Firs, The. *And* —5G **21**
Fisher Clo. *And* —5D **22**
Five Bridges Rd. *Win* —4A **16**
Fivefields Clo. *Win* —6E **13**
Fivefields Rd. *Win* —6E **13**
Fleming Rd. *Win* —2G **11**
Flensburg Clo. *And* —2H **21**
Flinders Clo. *And* —4F **23**
Flint Clo. *And* —1C **24**
Floral Way. *And* —1B **24**
Florence Ct. *And* —2B **22**
(in two parts)
Flowerdew Ct. *And* —1F **25**
Flowerdown Barrows. —1G 11
Flowerdown Cvn. Pk. *Win* —6G **3**
Focus 303 Bus. Cen. *And* —4E **23**
Focus Way. *And* —4D **22**
Folly Roundabout, The. *And* —4A **22**
Forbes Rd. *King W* —3D **4**
Fordington Av. *Win* —5H **11**
Fordington Rd. *Win* —5A **12** (1A **26**)
Forest La. *P Twen* —6F **23**
(in two parts)
Forge Fld. *And* —4B **22**
Foundry Rd. *Anna V* —3A **24**
Foxcotte. —2E 21
Foxcotte Clo. *Charl* —3F **21**
Foxcotte La. *Charl* —2E **21**
Foxcotte Rd. *Charl* —2E **21**
Fox La. *Win* —2G **15**
Frampton Way. *King W* —4E **5**
Francis Gdns. *Win* —3D **12**
Franklin Rd. *Twy* —2G **19**
Fraser Rd. *King W* —3D **4**
Friarsgate. *Win* —5C **12** (2E **26**)
Fromond Rd. *Win* —2G **11**
Froxfield Clo. *Win* —1H **11**
Fry Sq. And —3B 22
(off Cricketers Way)
Fulflood. —5B 12
Fulflood Ct. *Win* —5A **12** (1A **26**)
Fullerton Rd. *Up Cl & Good C* —6A **24**
Furley Clo. *Win* —5D **12**
Fyfield Way. *Win* —6F **3**

Gainsborough Ct. *And* —4H **21**
Galahad Clo. *And* —3A **22**
Gales Ct. *And* —5A **22**
Galileo Pk. *And* —4E **21**
Gallaghers Mead. *And* —5E **21**
Garbett Rd. *Win* —5E **13**
Garden Clo. *And* —5B **22**
Garden La. *Win* —5C **12** (2E **26**)
Garnier Rd. *Win* —2B **16**
Gar St. *Win* —6B **12** (3C **26**)
Gatekeeper Clo. *Win* —5E **13**
Gawaine Clo. *And* —1A **22**
General Johnson Ct. *Win* —1G **15**
Genoa Ct. *And* —1B **22**
(in two parts)
George Eyston Dri. *Win* —1H **15**
George Yd. *And* —6B **22**
George Yd., The. *Alr* —3F **9**
Georgia Clo. *And* —1B **24**
Gilberts Mead Clo. *Anna V* —3A **24**
Gillingham Clo. *King W* —4E **5**
Gladstone St. *Win* —5B **12** (1C **26**)
Glebelands. *Good C* —5F **25**
Glen Clo. *And* —5G **21**
Goch Way. *Charl* —3G **21**
Goddards Mead. *And* —6G **21**
Goddard Sq. And —3C 22
(off Cricketers Way)
Godson Ho. *Win* —2E **26**
Godwin Clo. *Win* —2G **11**
Godwins Fld. *Comp* —1C **18**
Goldfinch Way. *S Won* —1D **2**
Goodworth Clatford. —6E 25
Goodworth Vw. *Good C* —6E **25**
Gordon Av. *Win* —1E **17**
Gordon Rd. *Win* —5C **12** (1E **26**)
Goring Fld. *Win* —4G **11**
Grace Sq. *And* —3C **22**
Grafton Rd. *Win* —1B **16**
Granada Pl. *And* —4C **22**
Grange Clo. *Alr* —4E **9**
Grange Clo. *Win* —3A **16**
Grange Rd. *Alr* —4E **9**
Grange Rd. *Win* —4A **16**
Granville Pl. *Win* —1D **16**
Graveney Sq. And —3B 22
(off Cricketers Way)
Grayshott Clo. *Win* —1H **11**
Gt. Field Rd. *Win* —2H **11**
Gt. Minster St. *Win* —6C **12** (3D **26**)
Great Weir. *Alr* —2F **9**
Greenacres Dri. *Ott* —6C **18**
Green Clo. *Old Al* —1F **9**
Green Clo. *S Won* —1D **2**
Green Clo. *Win* —6C **4**
Greenhaven Clo. *And* —6C **22**
Greenhill Av. *Win* —5A **12**
Greenhill Clo. *Win* —5H **11**
Greenhill Rd. *Win* —6H **11** (1A **26**)
Greenhill Ter. *Win* —5A **12**
Grn. Jacket Clo. *Win* —2A **16**
Grn. Meadows La. *Good C* —5E **25**
Grn. Park Clo. *Win* —3D **12**
Green, The. *Charl* —3G **21**
Greenwich Way. *And* —3A **22**
Greyfriars. *Win* —2F **26**
Grosvenor Dri. *Win* —3D **12**
Grovelands Rd. *Win* —4F **11**
Grove Rd. *Shaw* —4C **18**
Groves Clo. *S Won* —1B **2**
Grove, The. *Pen M* —1B **20**
Guildhall Gallery. —6C 12 (3E 26)
Gurkha Mus., The. —6B 12 (3B 26)

Hackwood Clo. *And* —6F **21**
Hadrian Rd. *And* —2B **22**
Haig Rd. *Alr* —3F **9**
Haig Rd. *And* —5G **21**
Halifax Clo. *And* —4H **21**
Halls Farm Clo. *Win* —2A **12**
Hall Way, The. *Win* —6F **3**
Hambledon Clo. *Win* —1H **11**
Hamburg Clo. *And* —2H **21**
Hammond's Pas. *Win* —3C **26**
Hampton La. *Win* —4G **11**
Hanging Bushes La. *W'hll* —3B **20**
Hanover Clo. *And* —1B **24**
Hanover Ho. And —6B 22
(off London St.)
Hanover Lodge. *Win* —1B **16**
Hanson Rd. *And* —4G **21**
Hardyfair Clo. *W'hll* —3A **20**
Hare La. *Twy* —5G **19**
Harestock. —1G 11
Harestock Clo. *Win* —6H **3**
Harestock Rd. *Win* —2G **11**
Harewood Mobile Home Pk. *And* —4F **23**
Harroway La. *Pen H & And* —2C **20**
Harrow Down. *Win* —3H **15**
Harrow Way. *And* —3C **20**
(Hopkinson Way)
Harrow Way. *And* —4F **21**
(Upper Drove)
Harvest Clo. *Win* —3H **15**
Harwood Pl. *King W* —3E **5**
Hasted Dri. *Alr* —5E **9**
Hatherley Rd. *Win* —4A **12** (1A **26**)
Hattem Pl. *And* —3H **21**
Hawke Clo. *And* —4D **22**
Hawthorn Clo. *Alr* —4F **9**
Haydn Clo. *King W* —3D **4**
Hazel Clo. *And* —1B **24**
Hazeldene Gdns. *It Ab* —4E **7**
Hazeley Rd. *Twy* —3G **19**
Hazel Gro. *Win* —2H **15**
Headbourne Worthy Ho. *Win* —6D **4**
Heather Dri. *And* —4H **21**
Heath Va. *And* —6B **22**
Hedge End Rd. *And* —1F **25**
Helford Ct. *And* —3C **22**
Hendren Sq. *And* —3C **22**
Hengest Clo. *Charl* —2F **21**
Hepworth Clo. *And* —4A **22**
Heritage Ct. *Win* —2E **26**
Heron Ri. *And* —1F **25**
Hexagon, The. *And* —1B **24**
Hickory Dri. *Win* —1H **11**
Highbridge Rd. *Highb & Col C* —6F **19**
Highbury Rd. *Anna V* —3B **24**
Highcliffe Rd. *Win* —1D **16**
Highcroft. *Win* —6H **11**
Highfield. *Twy* —4G **19**
Highfield Av. *Twy* —4G **19**
Highfield Ter. *Win* —6A **12** (3B **26**)
Highlands Rd. *And* —6C **22**
Highmount Clo. *Win* —6D **12**
High St. *And* —6A **22**
High St. *Twy* —4G **19**
High St. *Win* —5B **12** (2C **26**)
(in three parts)
High Trees Dri. *Win* —3A **12**
Highways Rd. *Comp* —4C **18**
Hilden Way. *Win* —6E **3**
Hillbury Av. *And* —1C **24**
Hillier Way. *Win* —3C **12**
Hill Ri. *Twy* —3G **19**
Hillside. *Win* —6F **3**
Hillside Clo. *Win* —3G **11**
Hillside Rd. *Win* —4G **11**
Hillside Vs. *Charl* —3G **21**
Hill Ter. *Alr* —3F **9**
Hilltop. *Win* —6G **3**
Hinton Fields. *King W* —5E **5**
Hobbs Sq. And —3C 22
(off Cricketers Way)
Hockley Golf Course. —5C 16
Hockley Link. *Comp* —5A **16**
Hogarth Ct. *And* —3H **21**
Holdaway Clo. *King W* —4E **5**
Holland Dri. *And* —2H **21**
Hollands Clo. *Win* —6F **3**
Holly Wlk. *And* —1B **24**
Holmes Ct. *And* —6G **21**
Holm Oak Clo. *Win* —6E **3**
Home Farm Gdns. *Charl* —2F **21**
Home La. *Spar* —2A **10**
Homerise Ho. *Win* —1D **26**
Honeysuckle Clo. *Win* —3H **15**
Hood Clo. *And* —5D **22**
Hookpit Farm La. *King W* —3D **4**
Hopkinson Way. *And* —4D **20**
Hornbeam Clo. *S Won* —1D **2**
Hospital of St Cross, The. —3B 16
Hubert Rd. *Win* —3A **16**
Humberstone Rd. *And* —1E **25**
Hundred Acre Roundabout. *And* —5E **21**
Hunt Clo. *S Won* —1D **2**
Hunting Ga. *And* —5E **21**
Hurdle Way. *Comp* —1C **18**
Hussey Clo. *Win* —3C **12**
Hutton Sq. *And* —3C **22**
Hyde Abbey Rd. *Win* —5C **12** (1D **26**)
Hyde Church La. *Win* —4C **12**
Hyde Church Path. Win —4C 12
(off Hyde St.)
Hyde Clo. *Win* —4B **12** (1C **26**)
Hyde Ga. *Win* —4C **12** (1D **26**)
Hyde Ho. Gdns. *Win* —4C **12**
Hyde Lodge. *Win* —4B **12**
Hyde St. *Win* —5C **12** (1D **26**)

Icknield Way. *And* —1B **22**
Ilex Clo. *King W* —3D **4**
Imber Rd. *Win* —5E **13**
Itchen Abbas. —5E 7
Itchen Ct. *And* —3C **22**
Itchen Ct. *Win* —3F **26**
Itchen Stoke. —4A 8
Itchen Vw. *It Sto* —4A **8**
Ivy Clo. *Win* —2A **16**

Jacklyns Clo. *Alr* —5E **9**
Jacklyns La. *Alr* —5E **9**
Jardine Sq. And —3C 22
(off Cricketers Way)
Jellicoe Ct. And —4D 22
(off Admirals Way)
Jenson Gdns. *And* —6G **21**
Jervis Ct. *And* —4D **22**
Jesty Rd. *Alr* —5D **8**
Jewry St. *Win* —5C **12** (2C **26**)
Joule Rd. *And* —4D **20**
Junction Rd. *And* —4H **21**
Juniper Clo. *Win* —2H **15**
Jutland Cres. *And* —1H **21**

Keats Clo. *S Won* —1D **2**
Keats Clo. *Win* —3G **15**
Keble St. *Win* —1G **15**
Kellys Wlk. *And* —6G **21**
Kemmitt Way. *And* —1C **24**
Kenilworth Ct. Win —3C 12
(off Northlands Dri.)
Kennel La. *Win* —1F **11**
Kenyons Yd. *And* —5G **21**
Kerrfield. *Win* —6H **11**
(in two parts)
Kerrfield M. *Win* —6H **11**

Kestrel Clo. *Win* —3H **15**
Kew Wlk. *And* —6G **21**
Kiel Dri. *And* —2H **21**
Kilham La. *Win* —6E **11**
Kiln La. *Old Al* —1F **9**
Kimberley Clo. *Charl* —3G **21**
King Alfred Pl. *Win* —4C **12**
King Alfred's Statue. —3E 26
King Alfred Ter. *Win* —4C **12** (1D **26**)
King Arthur's Way. *And* —2A **22**
King Arthur's Way Roundabout. *And* —1B **22**
King George Rd. *And* —5F **21**
King Harold Ct. *Win* —1A **16**
Kings Av. *Win* —2A **16**
Kings Clo. *King W* —2D **4**
Kings Clo. *Twy* —2G **19**
Kingsdale Ct. *Win* —5B **12** (1C **26**)
Kingsgate Rd. *Win* —2B **16**
Kingsgate St. *Win* —1C **16**
Kings Head Yd. *Win* —6C **12** (3D **26**)
Kings La. *Win* —6G **13**
Kingsley Bungalows. *Alr* —5D **8**
Kingsley Pl. *Win* —2A **16**
Kingsmead. *Anna V* —3A **24**
Kings Mdw. *And* —6B **22**
Kings Rd. *Win* —1G **15**
King's Royal Hussar's Mus., The. —6B 12 (3B 26)
Kingstone Clo. *And* —1C **24**
Kings Wlk. *Win* —3E **26**
Kingsway. *And* —3E **23**
Kingsway Gdns. *And* —2A **22**
Kings Worthy. —5E 5
Kingsworthy Ct. *King W* —6E **5**
Kings Yd. *And* —5B **22**
Knight Clo. *Win* —3C **12**
Knights Enham. —1A 22
Knights Enham Roundabout. *And* —1A **22**
Kynegils Rd. *Win* —3H **11**

Laburnum Dri. *King W* —3D **4**
Ladies Wlk. *And* —1F **25**
Ladycroft. *Alr* —5C **8**
Lady Well La. *Alr* —2F **9**
Lainston Clo. *Win* —3G **11**
Laker Sq. *And* —3C **22**
Lakeside Clo. *Charl* —3F **21**
Lamb Clo. *And* —6C **22**
Lambourne Clo. *Spar* —2A **10**
Lamb Roundabout, The. *And* —6A **22**
Lancaster Clo. *And* —4H **21**
Landseer Ct. *And* —4H **21**
Langton Clo. *Win* —4A **12**
Langtons Ct. *Alr* —4G **9**
Lanham La. *Win* —6B **10**
(in three parts)
Lankhills Rd. *Win* —3B **12**
Lansdowne Av. *And* —1C **24**
Lansdowne Av. *Win* —2B **16**
Lansdowne Ct. *Win* —2B **16**
Lantern Ct. *Win* —1A **16**
Larch Clo. *King W* —2D **4**
Larch Dri. *And* —6E **21**
Larg Dri. *Win* —1G **11**
Lark Clo. *And* —3B **22**
Lark Hill Ri. *Win* —3H **15**
Larwood Sq. And —3C 22
(off Cricketers Way)
Launcelot Clo. *And* —2A **22**
Lawn Ho. *Win* —2E **26**
Lawn Rd. *Win* —6F **3**
Lawn St. *Win* —5C **12** (2E **26**)
Lawrence Clo. *And* —3H **21**
Lawrence Way. Win —3C 12
(off Worthy Rd.)
Legion La. *King W* —4D **4**
Leicester Pl. *And* —6A **22**
Leicester Way. *Win* —4E **13**
Leigh Clo. *And* —6C **22**
Leigh Gdns. *And* —6C **22**
Leigh Rd. *And* —6B **22**
Lent Hill Ct. *Win* —1H **15**
Leyton Way. *And* —1B **24**
Light Infantry Mus., The. —5B 12 (2B 26)
Lillywhite Cres. *And* —1B **22**
Lime Rd. *Alr* —4F **9**
Limetree Wlk. *Win* —5F **13**
Lime Wlk. *And* —1B **24**
Lindley Gdns. *Alr* —5F **9**
Lingen Clo. *And* —2A **22**
Links Rd. *Win* —4H **11**
Link, The. *And* —5E **21**
Linnets Rd. *Alr* —5E **9**
Linton Dri. *And* —4H **21**
Lions Hall. *Win* —6B **12** (4C **26**)
Lisle Clo. *Win* —4E **15**
Lisle Ct. *Win* —1A **16**
Litchfield Clo. *Charl* —2F **21**
Litchfield Rd. *Win* —1H **11**
Lit. Copse. *And* —1C **24**
Lit. Hayes La. *It Ab* —5F **7**
Lit. Minster St. *Win* —6C **12** (3D **26**)
Littleton. —1F 11
Littleton La. *Spar & Win* —1E **11**
Littleton Rd. *Win* —1F **11**
Livia Clo. *And* —1B **22**
Livingstone Rd. *And* —4E **23**
Loader Clo. *King W* —4E **5**
Lock's La. *Spar* —2A **10**
Lodge Clo. *And* —5G **21**
London Rd. *And* —6B **22**
London Rd. *And & And D* —5E **23**
London Rd. *Win & King W* —1D **12**
London St. *And* —6B **22**
Longbarrow Clo. *S Won* —1D **2**
Longfield Rd. *Win* —5E **13**
Longhouse Grn. *Win* —5E **13**
Longparish Ct. And —6B 22
(off London Rd.)
Long Park. —4C 2
Longstock Clo. *And* —6G **21**
Longstock Ct. And —6B 22
(off London Rd.)
Longstock Rd. *Good C* —6E **25**
Long Wlk. *Win* —2G **13**
Lovedon La. *King W* —2D **4**
Love La. *And* —6B **22**
Love La. *Twy* —4H **19**
Lovell Clo. *S Won* —1D **2**
Lovells Wlk. *Alr* —4E **9**
Loveridge Clo. *And* —1B **22**
Lovett Wlk. *Win* —2G **11**
Lovington La. *Avtn & Alr* —6H **7**
Lowden Clo. *Win* —3H **15**
Lwr. Brook St. *Win* —5C **12** (2E **26**)
Lower Rd. *S Won* —1B **2**
Lwr. Stanmore La. *Win* —2A **16**
Lowry Ct. *And* —4H **21**
Lubeck Dri. *And* —2H **21**
Lynch Clo. *Win* —3A **12**
Lyndhurst Clo. *Win* —1H **11**
Lynford Av. *Win* —3A **12**
Lynford Way. *Win* —3A **12**
Lynn Way. *King W* —5E **5**
Lynwood Ct. *Win* —3B **12**
Lynwood Dri. *And* —5G **21**

Macadam Way. *And* —4D **20**
Macklin Ho. *Win* —3A **26**
Madrid Rd. *And* —4C **22**
Magdalen Hill. *Win* —6D **12** (3F **26**)
Magdalen M. *Win* —3F **26**
Magellan Clo. *And* —4E **23**
Magnolia Clo. *And* —6G **21**
Main Rd. *Ott & Comp* —6B **18**
Main Rd. *Win* —5E **3**
Majorca Av. *And* —4C **22**
Makins Ct. *Alr* —4E **9**
Mallard Clo. *Alr* —3F **9**
Mallard Clo. *And* —3B **22**
Mall, The. And —6A 22
(off Bridge St.)
Malmesbury Gdns. *Win* —3H **11**
Malpass Rd. *Wor D* —1G **3**
Malthouse Clo. *Estn* —6H **5**
Manningford Clo. *Win* —2C **12**
Manor Clo. *Win* —5D **12**
Manor Copse. *And* —1B **22**
Mnr. Farm Grn. *Twy* —4F **19**
Manor Ri. *Anna V* —3C **24**
Manor Rd. *And* —4H **21**
Manor Rd. *Twy* —4F **19**
Mant's La. *Win* —6D **12** (4F **26**)
Maple Clo. *Alr* —5E **9**
Maple Dri. *King W* —3D **4**
Maple Wlk. *And* —1B **24**
Marchant Rd. *And* —6G **21**
March Clo. *And* —4B **22**
Market La. *Win* —6C **12** (3D **26**)
Market St. *Win* —6C **12** (3D **26**)
Mark La. *P Cnr & And* —4C **20**
(in two parts)
Markson Rd. *S Won* —1B **2**
Marlborough St. *And* —5A **22**
Marshall Sq. And —3C 22
(off Cricketers Way)
Marston Ga. *Win* —5C **12** (1D **26**)
Marsum Clo. *And* —1A **22**
Martins Fields. *Comp* —1C **18**
Martin Way. *And* —3B **22**
Martyr Worthy. —5B 6
Matilda Pl. *Win* —5C **12** (1D **26**)
May Tree Clo. *Win* —3G **15**
May Tree Rd. *And* —4F **21**
Mead Clo. *And* —6H **21**
Mead Hedges. *And* —1C **24**
Mead Hedges Footpath. *And* —6H **21**
Meadow Clo. *Alr* —4F **9**
Meadowcroft Clo. *Ott* —6C **18**
Meadowland. *King W* —4D **4**
Meadow Way. *And* —5F **21**
Meadow Way. *Win* —3G **15**
Mead Rd. *And* —6H **21**
Mead Rd. *Win* —3A **16**
Mead Vw. *Good C* —6E **25**
Meliot Ri. *And* —1A **22**
Melrose Ct. *Win* —1B **16**
Merchants Pl. *Win* —5C **12** (2E **26**)
Mercia Av. *Charl* —2F **21**
Meriden Ct. Win —3C 12
(off Northlands Dri.)
Mersey Ct. *And* —3C **22**
Meryon Rd. *Alr* —5E **9**
Mews Ct. *Ott* —6B **18**
Mews La. *Win* —6A **12** (3A **26**)
Micheldever Rd. *And* —6B **22**
Middle Brook St. *Win* —6C **12** (3E **26**)
(in two parts)
Middle Rd. *Win* —5A **12** (1A **26**)
Middleway, The. *And D & Longp* —4H **23**
Mildmay Ct. *Win* —3F **26**
Mildmay St. *Win* —2H **15**
Milland Rd. *Win* —1D **16**
Millers La. *Win* —4C **14**
Mill Hill. *Alr* —3F **9**
Mill La. *Abb W* —5F **5**
Mill La. *Bish S* —4H **9**
Millstream Clo. *And* —1D **24**
Millway Clo. *And* —6G **21**
Millway Rd. *And* —6G **21**
Milner Pl. *Win* —1A **16**
Milnthorpe La. *Win* —6A **12** (4A **26**)
Milton Av. *And* —4F **21**
Milverton Rd. *Win* —5H **11**
Mimosa Ct. *And* —1B **24**
Minden Clo. *And* —2A **22**
Minden Way. *Win* —2G **15**
Minstead Clo. *Win* —1H **11**
Minster La. *Win* —6C **12** (3D **26**)
Mint Yd. *Win* —3D **26**
Mitchell Clo. *And* —4D **20**
Mitford Rd. *Alr* —4D **8**
Momford Rd. *Win* —4F **15**
Monarch Way. *Win* —1G **15**
Moneyer Rd. *And* —2H **21**
Monks Rd. *Win* —4C **12**
Monmouth Sq. *Win* —1F **15**
Montgomery Clo. *Win* —2G **15**
Monxton Rd. *And* —6B **20**
(in two parts)
Monxton Rd. Roundabout. *And* —5D **20**
Moor Ct. La. *Spar* —2A **10**
Moore Clo. *And* —4A **22**
Moorside. *Win* —2F **26**
Moorside Rd. *Win* —4E **13**
Moot Clo. *And* —1B **22**
Morestead Rd. *Win* —2D **16**
(in two parts)
Mornington Clo. *And* —2E **25**
Mornington Dri. *Win* —3G **11**
Mortimer Clo. *King W* —5D **4**
Moss Rd. *Win* —5D **12**
Mountbatten Ct. *Win* —2A **12**
Mountbatten Pl. *King W* —3E **5**
Mount Clo. *Win* —2A **12**
Mt. Pleasant. *King W* —5D **4**
Mt. View Rd. *Win* —3F **15**
Munnings Ct. *And* —4H **21**
Murray Clo. *And* —2D **24**
Museum of the Iron Age, The. —5B 22
Mylen Bus. Cen. *And* —5G **21**
Mylen Rd. *And* —5G **21**

Napier Wlk. *And* —4D **22**
Nations Hill. *King W* —4D **4**
Nelson Rd. *Win* —6E **13**
Nelson Wlk. *And* —4D **22**
Nestor Clo. *And* —4H **21**
Neville Clo. *And* —1F **25**
Newall Rd. *And* —6C **20**
Newburgh St. *Win* —5B **12** (1B **26**)
Newbury La. *Pen M* —2C **20**
Newbury Rd. *And* —1A **22**
Newbury St. *And* —5B **22**
Newcomb Clo. *And* —2D **24**
New Farm Ind. Est. *Alr* —5D **8**
New Farm Rd. *Alr* —4D **8**
New Rd. *Win* —5F **3**
New St. *And* —3B **22**
Newton Rd. *Twy* —2G **19**
Newtown Clo. *And* —6G **21**
Nicholson Pl. *Alr* —4D **8**
Nickel Clo. *Win* —5D **12**
Nightingale Clo. *Win* —1F **15**
Norlands Dri. *Ott* —5C **18**
Norman Ct. La. *Up Cl* —2D **24**
Norman Rd. *Win* —1B **16**
Normans Flats. *Win* —1B **16**
Northbrook Av. *Win* —6D **12**
Northbrook Clo. *Win* —6E **13**
Northbrook Ct. *Win* —6E **13**
North Dri. *Win* —6F **3**
Northern Av. *And* —4A **22**
North Fields. *Twy* —2G **19**
N. Hill Clo. *Win* —3B **12**
N. Hill Ct. *Win* —4B **12**
Northington Rd. *It Ab* —4F **7**
Northlands Dri. *Win* —3C **12**
North Rd. *King W* —2D **4**
North Vw. *Win* —5A **12** (1A **26**)
North Walls. *Win* —5C **12** (1D **26**)
North Way. *And* —3D **22**
Nuns Rd. *Win* —4C **12**
Nuns Wlk. *Win* —4C **12**
(in two parts)
Nursery Gdns. *Win* —5H **11**
Nursery Rd. *Alr* —4F **9**
Nurse's Path. *Twy* —3G **19**
Nutbane Clo. *And* —6G **21**

Oak Bank. *And* —1E **25**
Oak Hill. *Alr* —5F **9**
Oaklands. *S Won* —1C **2**
Oaklands Clo. *Win* —1F **15**
Oakwood Av. *Ott* —6C **18**
Oakwood Clo. *Ott* —5C **18**
Octavia Hill. *Win* —1H **15**
Oglander Rd. *Win* —3C **12**
Olaf Clo. *And* —1B **22**
Old Alresford. —1F 9
Old Down Rd. *And* —4H **21**
Oldenburg Clo. *And* —2H **21**
Old English Dri. *And* —1H **21**
Old Gdns. *Win* —3B **12**
Old Hillside Rd. *Win* —4G **11**
Old Kennels Clo. *Win* —4E **15**
Old Kennels La. *Win* —4E **15**
Old Parsonage Ct. *Ott* —6C **18**
Old Rectory Gdns. *Abb W* —5F **5**
Old Rectory La. *Twy* —2G **19**
Old Stable M. *Win* —5E **3**
Old Station App. *Win* —6D **12** (3F **26**)
Old Station Rd. *It Ab* —5E **7**
Old Winton Rd. *And* —6B **22**
Oliver's Battery. —3F 15
Oliver's Battery Cres. *Win* —3F **15**
Oliver's Battery Gdns. *Win* —4F **15**
Oliver's Battery Rd. N. *Win* —2F **15**
Oliver's Battery Rd. S. *Win* —4F **15**
Orchard Clo. *Alr* —5F **9**
Orchard Clo. *S Won* —1B **2**
Orchard Rd. *And* —4G **21**
Orchard Rd. *S Won* —1B **2**
Orchard Wlk. *Win* —1D **26**
(Jewry St.)
Orchard Wlk. *Win* —3H **11**
(Stoney La.)
Orient Dri. *Win* —2G **11**
Osborne Rd. *And* —6H **21**
Otterbourne. —6B 18
Otterbourne Golf Cen. —4A 18
Otterbourne Ho. *Ott* —6B **18**
Otterbourne Ho. Gdns. *Ott* —6B **18**
Otterbourne Rd. *Comp* —1D **18**
Otterbourne Rd. *Shaw* —3D **18**
Oval, The. *And* —2C **22**
Owens Rd. *Win* —4B **12**
Ox Drove. *And & Pic P* —4F **23**
Ox Drove Ri. *Pic P* —2H **23**
Ox Drove Way. *Old Al* —1G **9**

Paddock Clo. *S Won* —1D **2**
Paddock, The. *King W* —5E **5**

Paddock Way. Alr —5E 9
Painters Fld. Win —3A 16
Palmer Dri. And —5D 22
Palmerston Ct. Win —2B 16
Palm Hall Clo. Win —6E 13
Parchment St. Win —6C 12 (3D 26)
(in two parts)
Park Av. Win —5C 12 (1E 26)
Park Clo. Win —3C 12
Park Ct. Win —3C 12
Park Ho. Win —1E 26
Park La. Abb W —5F 5
Park La. Twy —4G 19
Park Mt. Alr —3E 9
Park Rd. Win —3B 12
Parkside Gdns. Win —3G 11
Park Vw. Shaw —3E 19
Parkview Clo. And —3G 21
Parliament Pl. Win —3G 15
Parmiter Ho. Win —2F 26
Partridge Down. Win —4F 15
Pastures, The. King W —2D 4
Paternoster Ho. Win —3E 26
Paternoster Row. Win —6C 12 (3E 26)
Pattinson Cres. And —6C 20
Paulet Pl. Win —2A 16
Peacock Pl. Win —5E 13
Pearman Dri. And —5D 22
Pembroke Ct. And —5B 22
Pemerton Rd. Win —2H 11
Pen Clo. And —5C 22
Peninsula Rd. Win —6A 12 (4A 26)
Peninsula Sq. Win —6B 12 (3B 26)
Pentice, The. Win —3D 26
Penton Corner. —4C 20
Penton Grafton. —2B 20
Penton La. Cla —1B 20
Penton Mewsey. —1C 20
Penton Pl. Win —1D 16
Penton Rd. Twy —2G 19
Perins Clo. Alr —5D 8
Petersfield Rd. Win —6D 12
(in two parts)
Picket Piece. —2G 23
Picket Twenty. And & P Twen —5E 23
Picton Rd. And —2D 24
Pilgrims Ga. Win —4A 12 (1A 26)
Pilgrims Ho. Win —4A 12
Pilgrims Way. And —4C 22
Pine Clo. S Won —1D 2
Pine Clo. Win —4F 15
Pines, The. And —5H 21
Pine Wlk. And —1B 24
Pitt. —2E 15
Pitter Clo. Win —6F 3
Pitts La. And —1E 25
Place La. Comp —1D 18
Plantation Rd. And —6G 21
Plough Way. Win —3H 15
Plover Clo. And —3B 22
Plovers Down. Win —4F 15
Poets Way. Win —5H 11
Porchester Clo. Charl —2F 21
Portal Clo. And —6D 20
Portal Rd. Win —1D 16
Porters Clo. And —4F 21
Portland Gro. And —5A 22
Port La. Hurs —6B 14
Portway Clo. And —5F 21
Portway Ind. Est. And —4E 21
(East Portway)
Portway Ind. Est. And —4D 20
(Hopkinson Way)
Portway Roundabout. And —3E 21
Pound Hill. Alr —3E 9
Pound Rd. King W —3E 5
Poynters Clo. And —3H 21
Prince Albert Gdns. And —6A 22
(off Western Rd.)
Prince Clo. And —3D 22
Prince's Bldgs. Win —2E 26
Prince's Pl. Win —2A 16
Princess Ct. Win —5C 12 (1D 26)
Prinstead Clo. Win —1D 16
Printers Row. Win —2C 26
Priors Barton. Win —2B 16
Priors Dean Rd. Win —1H 11
Priors Way. Win —4F 15
Prospect Rd. Alr —5D 8
Pudding La. Win —6D 4

Quarry Rd. Win —6D 12 (4F 26)
Queens Av. And —5H 21
Queens Mead. Win —1G 15
Queen's Rd. Win —6H 11
Queen St. Twy —3F 19
Queensway. And —3D 22

Rack Clo. And —5B 22
Ramparts, The. And —1C 24
Ramsay Rd. King W —4E 5
Rances Way. Win —2A 16
Ranelagh Rd. Win —1B 16
Rank, The. W'hll —3A 20
Recreation Rd. And —5B 22
Rectory La. It Ab —3G 7
Rectory Pl. W'hll —3A 20
Reculver Way. Charl —2F 21
Redbridge Dri. And —6H 21
Redon Way. And —3G 21
Red Post La. And —6B 20
Red Post La. W'hll —4A 20
Red Rice Rd. Up Cl —6A 24
Rees Rd. Wor D —1G 3
Regent Clo. Ott —5C 18
Regent Ct. Win —3C 12
(off Northlands Dri.)
Regents Ct. And —4E 23
Reith Way. And —4D 20
Rewlands Dri. Win —2G 11
Reynolds Ct. And —3H 21
Rhodes Sq. And —2C 22
Richard Moss Ho. Win —1D 26
Richborough Dri. Charl —2E 21
Richmond Pk. Ott —5D 18
Ridgeway. Win —2G 15
Riley Rd. Wor D —1A 4
Ringlet Way. Win —5E 13
River Pk. Leisure Cen. —4C 12
Riverside. Good C —5E 25
Riverside Ho. Win —2F 26
Riverside Indoor Bowl Club. —4C 12
River Way. And —3B 22
Roberts Clo. King W —2D 4
Robertson Rd. Alr —5E 9
Robin Way. And —3B 22
Rockbourne Rd. Win —1H 11
Rodney Ct. And —4D 22
Roman Rd. Twy —3G 19
Roman's Rd. Win —1B 16
Roman Way. And —1B 22
Romsey Rd. Good C & Cot —6G 25
Romsey Rd. Win —3C 14 (3A 26)
Ronald Bowker Ct. Win —5A 12
Rooksbury Rd. And —1C 24
Rooks Down Rd. Win —2H 15
Rosebery Rd. Alr —4E 9
Rosemary Clo. Win —5D 12 (2F 26)
Rosewarne Ct. Win —4C 12 (1D 26)
Roundhuts Ri. Win —5E 13
Roundway Ct. And —5G 21
Rowan Clo. S Won —1D 2
Rowlings Rd. Win —2H 11
Royal Green Jackets Mus., The. —5B 12 (2B 26)
Royal Hampshire Regiment Mus., The. —6B 12 (3C 26)
Royal Oak Pas. Win —2D 26
Royal Winchester Golf Course. —5F 11
Royce Clo. And —4D 20
Roydon Clo. Win —2A 16
Rozelle Clo. Win —6E 3
Ruffield Clo. Win —3G 11
Rune Dri. And —1H 21
Russell Rd. Win —3C 12
Russet Clo. Alr —5E 9
Ryon Clo. And —1A 22

Sainsbury Clo. And —1D 24
St Annes Clo. Good C —6D 24
St Annes Clo. Win —2G 15
St Ann's Clo. And —6H 21
(in two parts)
St Bede's Ct. Win —4C 12
St Catherine's Hill Fort. —3C 16
St Catherine's Hill Nature Reserve. —3C 16
St Catherine's Rd. Win —1D 16
St Catherine's Vw. Win —2D 16
St Catherines Way. Chilc —2E 17
St Clement St. Win —6B 12 (3C 26)
St Clements Yd. Win —3C 26
St Cross Ct. Win —2B 16
St Cross Mede. Win —3A 16
St Cross Rd. Win —4A 16
St Faith's Rd. Win —2B 16
St George's St. Win —5C 12 (2D 26)
(in two parts)
St Giles Clo. Win —6D 12 (4F 26)
St Giles Hill. Win —6D 12 (3F 26)
St Hubert Rd. And —6G 21
St James' La. Win —6A 12 (3A 26)
St James' Ter. Win —6B 12 (3B 26)
St James' Vs. Win —6B 12 (4B 26)
St John's Rd. And —5B 22
St John's Rd. Win —5D 12
St John's St. Win —6D 12 (3F 26)
St Leonards Clo. S Won —1C 2
St Leonard's Rd. Win —1E 17
St Martin's Clo. Win —5D 12 (2F 26)
St Martins Trade Pk. Win —4D 12 (1F 26)
St Mary Magdalen Almshouses. Win —6D 12 (4F 26)
St Mary's Clo. King W —6E 5
St Marys Ter. Twy —3G 19
St Mary St. Win —2H 15
St Matthew's Rd. Win —3H 11
St Michael's Gdns. Win —6B 12 (4C 26)
St Michael's Pas. Win —1C 16
St Michael's Rd. Win —1B 16 (4C 26)
St Nicholas Ri. King W —5D 4
St Paul's Ct. Win —2C 26
St Paul's Hill. Win —5B 12 (1B 26)
St Paul's Pl. Win —5B 12
St Peter's Clo. Good C —5F 25
St Peter St. Win —5C 12 (2D 26)
(in two parts)
St Stephen's Rd. Win —3H 11
St Swithuns Ter. Win —6B 12 (4C 26)
St Swithun St. Win —6B 12 (4C 26)
St Swithuns Vs. Win —6C 12 (4D 26)
St Thomas Clo. Charl —2G 21
St Thomas' Pas. Win —6B 12 (3C 26)
St Thomas St. Win —6B 12 (4C 26)
Salcot Rd. Win —3C 12
Salisbury Rd. Alr —4E 9
Salmond Rd. And —5D 20
Salters Acres. Win —2G 11
Salters La. Win —3F 11
Sam Whites Hill. Up Cl —3C 24
Sandringham Ho. And —2A 22
(off Atholl Ct.)
Saor M. And —5H 21
Sarum Clo. Win —6G 11
Sarum Rd. Win —6B 10
Sarum Vw. Win —6F 11
Savoy Clo. And —6B 22
Sawyer Clo. Win —4F 11
Saxon Ct. And —2A 22
Saxon Rd. Win —4C 12
Saxon Way. And —2H 21
Scamblers Mead. Pen G —2B 20
Sceptre Ct. Wal I —4E 23
School La. It Ab —4F 7
School La. Win —6C 4
School Rd. Twy —3F 19
Scott Clo. And —4E 23
Scrubbs La. Bish S —6H 9
Searles Clo. Alr —4F 9
Segars La. Twy —4F 19
Selborne Pl. Win —2H 15
Seldon Clo. Win —3F 15
Sermon Rd. Win —4F 11
Seville Cres. And —4C 22
(in two parts)
Shackleton Sq. And —2C 22
(off Cricketers Way)
Shakespeare Av. And —4F 21
Shaw Clo. And —5E 21
Shawford. —2D 18
Shawford Rd. Shaw —3E 19
Sheddon Pl. Spar —3B 10
Sheep Fair. And —5C 22
Sheep Fair Clo. And —5C 22
Shelley Clo. It Ab —5E 7
Shelley Clo. Win —5H 11
Shepherds Clo. Win —3F 15
Shepherds Down. Alr —5E 9
Shepherds La. Comp —3A 18
Shepherds Rd. Win —5E 13
Shepherds Row. And —6C 22
Shepherds Spring La. And —5A 22
Sheppard Sq. And —3C 22
(off Cricketers Way)
Sherbrooke Clo. King W —3E 5
Sheridan Clo. Win —2G 15
Shipley Rd. Twy —2G 19
Short La. P Cnr —4B 20
Sidmouth Rd. And —5C 22
Silchester Clo. And —3G 21
Silkstead La. Ott —2A 18
Silkweavers Rd. And —5B 22
Silverbirch Rd. And —4G 21
Silver Hill. Win —6C 12 (3E 26)
Silverwood Clo. Win —2H 15
Silwood Clo. Win —4H 11
Simonds Ct. Win —3C 12
Sleepers Delle Gdns. Win —1A 16
Sleepers Hill. —6G 11
Sleeper's Hill. Win —1G 15
Sleeper's Hill Gdns. Win —1H 15
Sleeper's Hill Ho. Win —1H 15
Slessor Clo. And —6D 20
Smannell Rd. And & Sman —2B 22
Smannell Rd. Roundabout. And —3A 22
Smeaton Rd. And —3D 20
Sobers Sq. And —2C 22
Soke, The. Alr —3F 9
Somers Clo. Win —2H 15
Somerville Ct. And —4D 22
Somerville Rd. King W —2E 5
Sopwith Pk. And —4D 20
South Clo. Alr —4D 8
South Down. —3D 18
Southdown Rd. Shaw —3D 18
South Dri. Win —1E 11
S. End Rd. And —1F 25
Southgate M. Win —6B 12 (4C 26)
Southgate St. Win —6B 12 (3C 26)
Southgate Vs. Win —4C 26
South Rd. Alr —4D 8
South St. And —1E 25
South Vw. Win —5A 12 (2A 26)
South Vw. Gdns. And —6B 22
Southview Pk. Homes. Win —4G 15
S. View Rd. Win —4F 15
South Way. And —3D 22
Southwick Clo. Win —1H 11
South Winchester Golf Course. —3E 15
South Wonston. —1C 2
Sparkford Clo. Win —1A 16
Sparkford Rd. Win —1A 16
Sparrowgrove. Ott —5C 18
Sparsholt. —2B 10
Sparsholt La. Win & Spar —5A 14
Spey Ct. And —3C 22
Spicers Ct. Win —5B 12 (1B 26)
Spinney Cvn. Pk., The. Alr —3E 9
Spinney, The. Comp —2C 18
Spitfire End. Win —5F 13
Spitfire Link. Win —6F 13
Springfield Clo. And —5D 22
Spring Gdns. Alr —5D 8
Spring M. And —4B 22
Springvale Av. King W —4D 4
Springvale Rd. Win —6D 4
Spring Way. Alr —5E 9
Spruce Clo. And —6E 21
Spruce Clo. S Won —1D 2
Square, The. Win —6C 12 (3D 26)
Stainers La. S Won —1B 2
(in two parts)
Standon. —5A 14
Stanham Clo. Wor D —1H 3
Stanmore. —2H 15
Stanmore La. Win —1G 15
Staple Gdns. Win —5B 12 (2C 26)
Statham Sq. And —2C 22
Station App. Alr —4F 9
Station App. And —5G 21
Station App. It Ab —4E 7
Station Clo. It Ab —4E 7
Station Hill. It Ab —5E 7
Station Hill. Win —5B 12 (1C 26)
Station Rd. Alr —3F 9
Station Rd. Win —5B 12 (1B 26)
Station Ter. Shaw —3E 19
Stavedown Rd. S Won —1B 2
Stephenson Clo. And —4E 21
Step Ter. Win —5A 12 (2A 26)
Sterling Pk. And —4E 21
Stiles Dri. And —5D 22
Stockbridge Rd. Good C —6A 24
Stockbridge Rd. Spar —4A 2 (1A 26)
Stockbridge Rd. Win —1E 11 (1A 26)
Stockers Av. Win —3H 11
Stockwell Pl. Spar —2B 10
Stoke Charity Rd. S Won & King W —1D 4
Stoke Rd. Win —2C 12
Stone Clo. And —1C 24
Stonemasons Ct. Win —2D 26
Stoney La. Win —3H 11
Stourhead Clo. And —6G 21
Stratford Ct. Win —3C 12
(off Northlands Dri.)
Strathfield Rd. And —2D 24

Stratton Rd. Win —6D 12
Stuart Ct. And —2A 22
Stuart Cres. Win —1A 16
Stubbs Ct. And —3H 21
Suffolk Rd. And —6H 21
Sun Hill Cres. Alr —5F 9
Sun La. Alr —5F 9
Sunnybank. Red P —6A 20
Sunnydown Rd. Win —4E 15
Sunnyside Clo. Charl —3F 21
Sussex St. Win —5B 12 (2C 26)
Sutcliffe Sq. And —2C 22
(off Cricketers Way)
Sutherland Ct. And —4A 22
(off Artists Way)
Sutton Gdns. Win —5C 12 (2D 26)
Swallowfields. And —2B 22
Swan La. Win —5B 12 (1C 26)
Swanmore Clo. Win —2G 11
Swift Clo. And —3B 22
Swift Clo. Win —2H 15
Sycamore Dri. King W —3D 4
Sycamore Wlk. And —1B 24
Symonds St. Win —6C 12 (4D 26)

Tanner St. Win —6C 12 (3E 26)
Taplings Clo. Win —2H 11
Taplings Rd. Win —2H 11
Taskers Dri. Anna V —2A 24
Tate Sq. And —2C 22
Taylors Corner. Win —6D 4
Technology Cen. & Intech. —6G 11
Tedder Clo. And —6D 20
Teg Down Meads. Win —4F 11
Telford Ga. And —4D 20
Temple Dri. Avtn —6E 7
Terrace, The. Estn —6A 6
Texas Dri. Win —5F 15
Thistledown Clo. And —4G 21
Thurmond Cres. Win —1G 15
Thurmond Rd. Win —1G 15
Tiberius Rd. And —2B 22
Tichborne Down. Alr —5E 9
Tilden Rd. Comp —4D 18
Tintagel Clo. And —2A 22
Toledo Gro. And —4C 22
Tollgate Rd. And —4F 21
Tourist Info. Cen. —6A 22
(Andover)
Tourist Info. Cen. —6C 12 (3E 26)
(Winchester)
Tovey Ct. And —4D 22
Tovey Pl. King W —4E 5
Tower Arts Cen., The. —1F 15
Tower Clo. Charl —2F 21
Tower Ct. Win —5B 12 (1C 26)
Tower Rd. Win —5B 12 (1C 26)
Tower St. Win —5B 12 (2C 26)
Town Sta. Roundabout. And —6A 22
Trafalgar St. Win —6B 12 (3C 26)
Trajan Wlk. And —2B 22
Traveller's End. Win —4H 11
Treble Clo. Win —3F 15
Trenchard Rd. And —5D 20
Trinity Ri. Pen M —1B 20
Trowbridge Ct. Win —2D 26
Trueman Sq. And —2C 22
(off Cricketers Way)
Trussell Clo. Win —2H 11
Trussell Cres. Win —2H 11
Tudor Ct. And —2A 22
Tudor Way. King W —3D 4
Turin Ct. And —1B 22
(in two parts)
Turner Ct. And —4H 21
Turnpike Down. Win —5E 13
Twford. —3G 19
Twyford Ct. Win —3C 12

Ullswater Gro. Alr —5F 9
Union St. And —5B 22
(off East St.)
Union St. Win —5D 12 (2F 26)
Uphill Rd. Win —6F 3
Uplands Rd. Win —2A 12
Up. Brook St. Win —6C 12 (3D 26)
(in three parts)
Upper Clatford. —3C 24
Upper Drove. And —5E 21
Up. High St. Win —5B 12 (1B 26)
Upton Grey Clo. Win —2H 11

Valdean Mobile Home Pk. Alr —3F 9
Valencia Way. And —4B 22
Vale Rd. Win —1E 17
Vale Way. King W —2D 4
Valley Ct., The. Win —1H 15
Valley Mead. Anna V —2A 24
Valley Ri. Up Cl —3C 24
Valley Rd. Win —6F 3
Valley, The. Win —1G 15
Venice Ct. And —2B 22
(in two parts)
Verden Way. And —2H 21
Verity Sq. And —2C 22
Vernham Rd. Win —3H 11
Vespasian Rd. And —2B 22
Vestry Clo. And —5H 21
Vian Pl. King W —3E 5
Victoria Ct. And —6H 21
Victoria Ga. Win —4B 12 (1C 26)
Victoria Rd. Win —4B 12 (1C 26)
Vigo Rd. And —5B 22
Vigo Rd. Roundabout. And —5B 22
Viking Way. And —1B 22
Village St. Good C —5E 25
Villiers Ct. Win —3C 26
Vincent Dri. And —6B 22
Viscount Ct. And —4E 23

Wales St. Win —5D 12 (2F 26)
Walk, The. Win —5B 12 (3B 26)
Walled Mdw. And —6B 22
Walnut Gro. Win —4H 11
Walnut Tree Clo. S Won —1C 2
Walnut Tree Rd. And —6H 21
Walpole Rd. Win —2G 15
Walton Pl. Win —2H 15
Walworth Enterprise Cen. And —4D 22
Walworth Ind. Est. And —3F 23
Walworth Rd. And & Pic P —4D 22
Walworth Roundabout. And —4D 22
Ward Clo. And —3A 22
Warner Ct. Win —3C 12
(off Northlands Dri.)
Warren Rd. Win —5E 13
Warwick Clo. Win —3B 12
Warwick Ct. Win —3C 12
(off Northlands Dri.)
Water Clo. Win —6C 12 (4E 26)
Watercress Mdw. Alr —5D 8
Water La. Abb W —6F 5
Water La. It Sto —4A 8
Water La. Win —6D 12 (3F 26)
Waterloo Ct. And —6A 22
Waterloo Ter. Anna V —3B 24
Watermills Clo. And —1D 24
Watersmeet. Win —4F 26
Waterworks Rd. Ott —5C 18
Watery La. And —4B 22
Watery La. Up Cl —3C 24
Watley La. Spar —2B 10
Watley La. Twy —3H 19
Watson Acre. And —5G 21
Watt Clo. And —4E 21
Wavell Way. Win —2G 15
Waverley Dri. S Won —1D 2
Waynflete Pl. Win —1G 15
Weavers Clo. And —5B 22
Webster Rd. Win —4F 11
Wedmore Clo. Win —4E 15
Weeke. —3H 11
Weeke Mnr. Clo. Win —3H 11
Weirs, The. Win —4F 26
Wellesley Ct. And —1E 25
Wellesley Rd. And —1E 25
Well Ho. La. Win —6A 4
Wellington Rd. And —4H 21
Welshers La. Comp —1C 18
Wentworth Grange. Win —1A 16
Wesley Rd. King W —4E 5
Wessex Dri. Win —3A 12
Wessex Gdns. And —5H 21
Westbrooke Clo. And —6A 22
W. End Clo. Win —5A 12 (2A 26)
W. End Ter. Win —5A 12 (2A 26)
Western Av. And —5A 22
Western Rd. And —6A 22
Western Rd. Win —5A 12 (1A 26)
W. Field Rd. King W —2E 5
Westfield Rd. Win —6F 3
Westgate, The. —2C 26
West Hayes. Win —6H 11
West Hill. —6B 12
W. Hill Dri. Win —5A 12
W. Hill Pk. Win —5H 11
W. Hill Rd. S Won —1D 2
W. Hill Rd. N. S Won —1D 2
W. Hill Rd. S. S Won —1D 2
Westley. —1A 10
Westley Clo. Win —4H 11
Westley La. Spar —1A 10
Westman Rd. Win —3H 11
Westmarch Bus. Cen. And —3B 22
Westminster Ga. Win —2F 15
West Portway. And —3D 20
West St. Alr —3F 9
West St. And —5A 22
Westview Rd. Win —3E 11
West Way. And —4D 22
Wetherby Gdns. Charl —3G 21
Weyhill. —3A 20
Weyhill Gdns. W'hll —4A 20
Weyhill Rd. And —5E 21
Wharf Hill. Win —1D 16
Wharf Mill. Win —1D 16
(off Wharf Hill)
Wheatland Clo. Win —2H 15
Whitehill La. Alr —5G 9
White La. Twy —1G 19
White Oak Way. Anna V —3A 24
Whiteshute La. Win —3H 15
(in two parts)
Whittle Rd. And —4D 20
Whynot La. And —5G 21
Wilberforce Clo. Win —1G 15
Willis Waye. King W —5D 4
Willow Gro. And —6H 21
Willows, The. And —1D 24
Winchester. —3A 12
Winchester By-Pass. Win & King W —4B 4
Winchester By-Pass. Wor D & Win —1F 3
Winchester Castle Great Hall. —6B 12 (3C 26)
Winchester Cathedral. —6C 12 (3D 26)
Winchester Cathedral Triforium Gallery. —6C 12 (4D 26)
Winchester City Mill. —6D 12 (3F 26)
Winchester Gallery. —5D 12 (1F 26)
Winchester Gdns. And —1F 25
Winchester Heritage Cen.
(off Heritage Ct.) —5C 12 (2E 26)
Winchester Rd. Alr —4C 8
Winchester Rd. And —6B 22
Winchester Rd. Comp —1D 18
Winchester Rd. Good C & Wher —6G 25
Windermere Gdns. Alr —5F 9
Windsor Ho. Win —2F 26
Windsor Rd. Alr —5E 9
Windsor Rd. And —5H 21
Winnall Clo. Win —4E 13
Winnall Mnr. Rd. Win —5E 13
Winnall Moors Nature Reserve. —5D 12 (1F 26)
Winnall Trad. Est. Win —4E 13
(Easton La.)
Winnall Trad. Est. Win —5E 13
(Winnall Valley Rd.)
Winnall Valley Rd. Win —5E 13
Winslade Rd. Win —1G 11
Winterdyne M. And —6H 21
Winton Chase. And —5C 22
Winton Clo. Win —3B 12
Wisley Rd. And —6F 21
Witan Clo. And —1B 22
Witton Hill. Alr —5E 9
Wolfe Clo. Win —2G 15
Wolversdene Clo. And —6C 22
Wolversdene Gdns. And —6C 22
Wolversdene Rd. And —6B 22
Wolvesey Castle. —6C 12 (4E 26)
Wolvesey Palace. —6C 12 (4E 26)
Wolvesey Ter. Win —1D 16
Woodfield Dri. Win —1F 15
Woodgreen Rd. Win —1H 11
Woodland Drove. Col C —6G 19
Woodlands Ct. Win —4C 12
Woodlands, The. King W —5E 5
Woodlands Way. And —5C 22
Woodlea Clo. Win —3A 12
Woodman Clo. Spar —3B 10
Woodman La. Spar —2B 10
Woodpeckers Dri. Win —3G 11
Woolford Clo. Win —1G 15
Wool Gro. And —6C 22
Woolley Sq. And —2C 22
Woolverton. Win —4H 11
Wordsworth Clo. Win —5H 11
Worrell Sq. And —2C 22
(off Cricketers Way)
Worthy La. Win —4B 12 (1C 26)
Worthy Rd. Win —4C 12
Wren Clo. Win —2H 15
Wrights Clo. S Won —1C 2
Wrights Way. S Won —1C 2
Wye Ct. And —3C 22
Wykeham Ind. Est., The. Win —3E 13
(in two parts)
Wykeham Pl. Win —1H 15
Wyndham Rd. And —1C 24

Yew Hill. —5E 15
Yew Tree Clo. Good C —6E 25
York Ct. And —2A 22

Other A-Z Publications

A-Z STREET ATLASES

Coloured ■ Black & White ❑

Aldershot ■ Bangor ■ Barnsley ■ Basingstoke ■ Birmingham ■❑ Birmingham Mini ■ Birmingham De Luxe ■ Blackburn/Burnley ■ Blackpool ■ Bolton ■ Bournemouth ■ Bracknell ■ Bradford ■ Brighton/Worthing ■ Bristol / Bath ■ Bristol / Bath Deluxe ■ Bromley ■ Burton upon Trent ■ Cambridge ■ Cannock ■ Cardiff/Newport ■ Chelmsford ■ Cheltenham/Gloucester/Stroud ■ Chester ■ Chichester/Bognor Regis ■ Colchester ■ Coventry/Rugby ■ Crawley ■ Croydon ■ Dartford ■ Derby ■ Doncaster ■ Eastbourne ■ Edinburgh ■ Exeter ■ Folkestone/Dover ■ Glasgow ■ Glasgow De Luxe ■ Guildford/Woking ■ Hamilton/Motherwell ■ Hatfield ■ Hemel Hempstead ■ Huddersfield ■ Ipswich ■ Leeds ■ Leeds/Bradford ■ Leicester ■ Lincoln ■ Liverpool ❑■ Liverpool De Luxe ■ London ❑■ "Big" London ■ London Large Format ■ London Mini ■ London De Luxe ❑ Inner London in Super Scale ■ London Atlas (Paper & Case) ■ Master Atlas of Greater London (Paper & Case) ■ London Motorists' Atlas ■ Loughborough ■ Luton / Dunstable ■ Maidstone/Chatham ■ Manchester ❑■ Manchester De Luxe ■ Manchester Mini ■ Mansfield ■ Margate/Ramsgate ■ Middlesbrough/Stockton ❑ Milton Keynes ■ Newbury ■ Newcastle upon Tyne / Sunderland / Durham ❑■ Northampton ■ Norwich ■ Nottingham ■ Nuneaton ■ Oldham/Rochdale ■ Oxford ■ Paisley ■ Peterborough ■ Plymouth ■ Portsmouth ■ Preston ■ Reading ■ Redditch ■ Reigate/Redhill ■ Richmond/Kingston upon Thames ■ Royal Tunbridge Wells / Tonbridge ■ St. Albans ■ Sheffield ■ Slough ■ Southampton ■ Southend ■ Southport ■ Stafford ■ Stratford upon Avon ■ Stevenage ■ Stoke-on-Trent ■ Swansea ■ Swindon ■ Torbay ■ Wakefied ■ Warrington ■ Watford ■ Weymouth / Dorchester ■ Wigan ■ Winchester ■ Wirral ■

A-Z STREET PLANS

Coloured ■ Black & White ❑

Barnet ❑ Bath ■ Bexley ❑ Birmingham Inner District ■ Bristol City Centre ■ Cambridge ■ Canterbury ■ Cheltenham ■ Chester ■ Coventry ■ Croydon ❑ Darlington ❑ Derby ❑ Durham ■ Ealing ❑ Exeter ■ Gloucester ■ Harrow ❑ Hartlepool ❑ Hayes ❑ Hounslow ❑ Ilford / Romford ❑ Lincoln ■ Liverpool / Birkenhead / Wallasey ❑ Manchester & Salford City Centres ❑ Newcastle upon Tyne Inner District ■ Northampton ■ Norwich ■ Oxford ■ Peterborough ■ Preston ❑ Reading ❑ Rotherham ❑ St. Helens ❑ Sheffield Inner District ❑ Slough ❑ Staines ❑ Stoke-on-Trent ❑ Stratford-upon-Avon ■ Sutton / Epsom ❑ Swansea ■ Swindon ■ Taunton ❑ Torbay ■ Walton-on-Thames ❑ Warrington ❑ Watford ❑ Wolverhampton ■

A-Z STREET ATLASES on CD ROM

Bristol & Bath ■ Glasgow ■ London ■ Greater London ■ Manchester ■ Tyne and Wear ■ West Yorkshire ■ West Midlands ■

A-Z ROAD ATLASES

Great Britain Road Atlas (Casebound & Spiral)
G.B. Road Atlas Super Scale/Spiral Bound
G.B. Road Atlas Large Format
Handy G.B. Road Atlas
Mini G.B.Road Atlas
■ Regional Road Atlases
South East England Road Atlas ■ Southern England Road Atlas ■ East Anglia Road Atlas ■ Devon & Cornwall Road Atlas ■ Wales Road Atlas
■ London Motorists' Atlas

A-Z ROAD & COUNTY MAPS

■ A-Z Gt. Britain Road Map Series:(5 miles to 1inch) ✶ S.E. and Central England ✶ S.W. England and S. Wales ✶ Wales and Central England ✶ Northern England ✶ Scotland (Reversible)
■ A-Z Gt. Britain Road Map Series: (3 miles to 1inch) **1.** Devon and Cornwall **2.** Southern England **3.** London Home Counties **4.** 50 Miles Around Bristol **5.** South Wales **6.** 50 Miles Around Birmingham **7.** East Anglia **8.** North Wales **9.** 50 Miles Around Manchester/Liverpool **10.** East Midlands **11.** Yorkshire and Humberside **12.** 50 Miles Around Newcastle upon Tyne **13.** Central Scotland
■ Great Britain Road Map (Reversible)
■ Great Britain Road Map
■ England and Wales Road Map
■ Motorways Map: England and Wales M25 / London (Reversible)
■ G.B. Counties & Unitary Authorities Map
■ 50 Miles Around London
■ 35 Miles Around London ✶ London to the S.E. Coast ✶ London to the South Coast ✶ Cotswolds & Chilterns ✶ Hampshire /Dorset/Wilts ✶ Kent County ✶ Surrey/E. Sussex/W. Sussex ✶
■ Visitors' Maps of: Devon ✶ Cornwall ✶ Isle of Wight ✶ Lake District ✶

A-Z COUNTY STREET ATLASES

Berkshire ■ Essex ■ Greater Manchester ■ Hertfordshire ■ Kent ■ Surrey ■ Tyne & Wear ■ West Midlands ■

A-Z TOWN MAPS Coloured

■ *Premier Street Map Series:* Birmingham ✶ Bournemouth ✶ Bradford ✶ Bristol ✶ Cardiff ✶ Edinburgh ✶ Glasgow ✶ Leeds ✶ Leicester ✶ Liverpool ✶ London ✶ Manchester ✶ Middlesbrough ✶ Newcastle upon Tyne ✶ Nottingham ✶ Plymouth ✶ Portsmouth ✶ Sheffield ✶ Southampton ✶ Sunderland ✶
■ *Main Road Map Series:* Birmingham ✶ London ✶ Manchester and Liverpool ✶
■ *Other London Street Maps:* 9 Sheet Master Maps of London ✶ 6" Map of Central London ✶ 9" Super Scale Map ✶ Visitors' London ✶ Handy Map of Central London ✶ Postcode Map of London

A-Z GUIDES

Visitors' London Atlas and Guide
London Handy Guide and Atlas

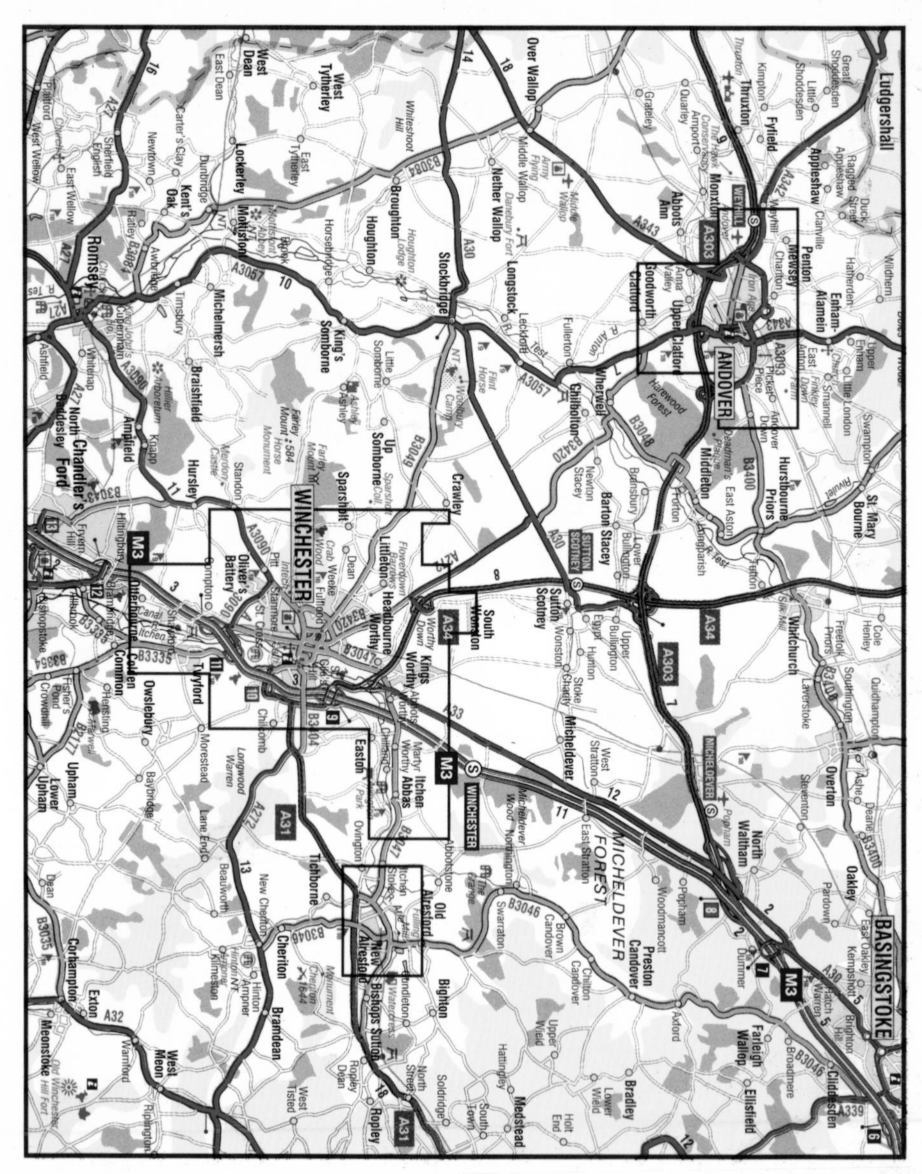

Geographers' A-Z Map Company Ltd

Head Office : (General Enquiries & Trade Sales)
Fairfield Road, Borough Green, Sevenoaks,
Kent TN15 8PP Telephone: 01732 781000

Showrooms : (Retail Sales)
44 Gray's Inn Road, London, WC1X 8HX
Telephone: 020 7440 9500

ISBN 0-85039-770-7

£2.75